Teaching Students to READ Like DETECTIVES

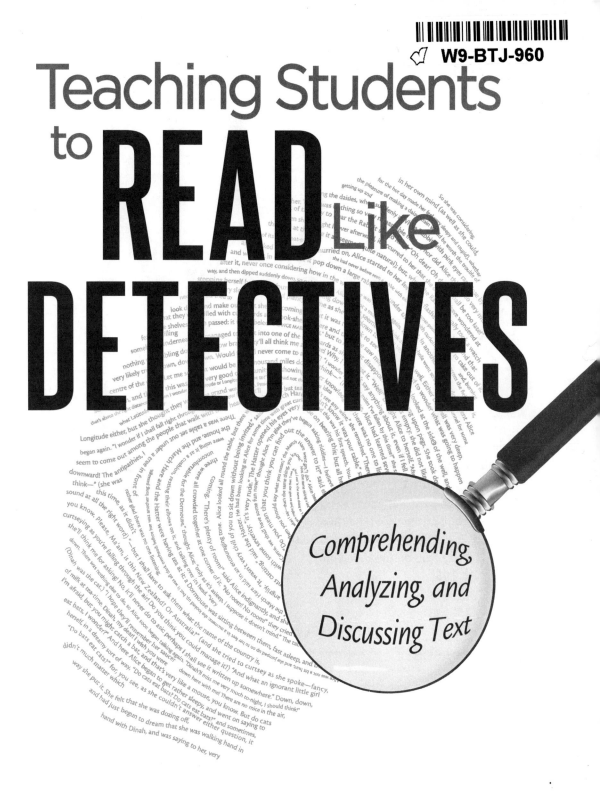

Comprehending, Analyzing, and Discussing Text

DOUGLAS FISHER   NANCY FREY   DIANE LAPP

Solution Tree | Press

a division of

Solution Tree

555 North Morton Street
Bloomington, IN 47404
800.733.6786 (toll free) / 812.336.7700
FAX: 812.336.7790

email: info@solution-tree.com
solution-tree.com
Printed in the United States of America

15 14 13 12 11   1 2 3 4 5

Library of Congress Cataloging-in-Publication Data

Fisher, Douglas, 1965-
 Teaching students to read like detectives : comprehending, analyzing, and discussing text / Douglas Fisher, Nancy Frey, Diane Lapp.
     p. cm.
 Includes bibliographical references and index.
  ISBN 978-1-935543-52-7 (perfect bound) -- ISBN 978-1-935543-53-4 (library edition) 1. Reading comprehension. 2. Discussion. I. Frey, Nancy, 1959- II. Lapp, Diane. III. Title.
  LB1573.7.F553 2012
  372.47'2--dc23
                            2011019670

Solution Tree
Jeffrey C. Jones, CEO & President

Solution Tree Press
President: Douglas M. Rife
Publisher: Robert D. Clouse
Vice President of Production: Gretchen Knapp
Managing Production Editor: Caroline Wise
Senior Production Editor: Risë Koben
Copy Editor: David Eisnitz
Text Designer: Raven Bongiani
Cover Designers: Amy Shock
                 Jenn Taylor

Acknowledgments

Solution Tree Press would like to thank the following reviewers:

Jan Miller Burkins
Independent Consultant, Executive
  Editor and Publisher
Literacyhead Magazine
Athens, Georgia

Kay Parks Haas
Instructional Projects Specialist—
  Secondary Focus
Olathe District Schools
Olathe, Kansas

Glenda Hinton
Reading Specialist
Barnaby Manor Elementary School
Oxon Hill, Maryland

C. Denise Kelly
Communications Arts Facilitator K–12
Springfield Public Schools
Springfield, Missouri

Deborah Kozdras
Instructor and Chief Creative Officer,
  Stavros Center for Economic
  Education
University of South Florida
Tampa, Florida

Ellen Surra Melocik
English Department Chair
Clovis West High School
Fresno, California

Julie Ray
Sixth- and Eighth-Grade Reading
  Teacher
Taylor Road Middle School
Johns Creek, Georgia

Marguerite C. Sneed
4–5 Learning Facilitator
Charles W. Nash Elementary School
Kenosha, Wisconsin

Jeffrey Zwiers
Instructor, Secondary Teacher Education
  Program
Stanford University
Stanford, California

Table of Contents

CHAPTER 5

About the Authors

Douglas Fisher, PhD, is professor of language and literacy education in the Department of Teacher Education at San Diego State University and a classroom teacher at Health Sciences High and Middle College. He teaches preservice courses in literacy and English language learners, graduate courses in reading instruction and intervention, and doctoral courses in policy, research, and literacy. As a classroom teacher, Dr. Fisher focuses on English language arts instruction. He was director of professional development for the City Heights Educational Collaborative and also taught English at Hoover High School.

Dr. Fisher received an International Reading Association Celebrate Literacy Award for his work on literacy leadership. For his work as codirector of the City Heights Professional Development Schools, Dr. Fisher received the Christa McAuliffe award. He was corecipient of the Farmer Award for excellence in writing from the National Council of Teachers of English for the article "Using Graphic Novels, Anime, and the Internet in an Urban High School," published in *The English Journal*.

Dr. Fisher has written numerous articles on reading and literacy, differentiated instruction, and curriculum design. His books include *Literacy 2.0: Reading and Writing in 21st Century Classrooms*, *Creating Literacy-Rich Schools for Adolescents*, *Checking for Understanding*, *Better Learning Through Structured Teaching*, and *Content-Area Conversations*.

He earned a bachelor's degree in communication, a master's degree in public health, an executive master's degree in business, and a doctoral degree in multicultural education. Dr. Fisher completed postdoctoral study focused on standards-based reforms at the National Association of State Boards of Education.

Nancy Frey, PhD, is a professor of literacy in the School of Teacher Education at San Diego State University. Through the university's teacher-credentialing and reading specialist programs, she teaches courses on elementary and secondary reading instruction and literacy in content areas, classroom management, and supporting students with diverse learning needs. Dr. Frey also teaches classes at Health Sciences High and Middle College in San Diego. She is a board member of the California Reading Association and a credentialed special educator and reading specialist in California.

Before joining the university faculty, Dr. Frey was a public school teacher in Florida. She worked at the state level for the Florida Inclusion Network helping districts design systems for supporting students with disabilities in general education classrooms.

She is the recipient of the 2008 Early Career Achievement Award from the National Reading Conference and the Christa McAuliffe Award for excellence in teacher education from the American Association of State Colleges and Universities. She was corecipient of the Farmer Award for excellence in writing from the National Council of Teachers of English for the article "Using Graphic Novels, Anime, and the Internet in an Urban High School."

Dr. Frey is coauthor of *Literacy 2.0: Reading and Writing in 21st Century Classrooms*, *Checking for Understanding*, *Better Learning Through Structured Teaching*, and *Content-Area Conversations*. She has written articles for *The Reading Teacher*, *Journal of Adolescent and Adult Literacy*, *English Journal*, *Voices in the Middle*, *Middle School Journal*, *Remedial and Special Education*, and *Educational Leadership*.

Diane Lapp, EdD, is a distinguished professor of education at San Diego State University and an English teacher and literacy coach at Health Sciences High and Middle College (HSHMC). Previously, she taught elementary and middle school grade levels. Dr. Lapp focuses on instruction that supports learning for a diverse range of students. Her career is founded on the idea that motivation and well-planned, guided instruction must be based on a continuous assessment of strengths and needs shown by the students.

Throughout her career as an educator and education professor, Dr. Lapp has been drawn to urban schools catering to children of poverty who are often misunderstood, misdiagnosed, mistreated, and uncared for because of unfamiliarity that exist between their families and their teachers. Combining her two current positions, Dr. Lapp established a high school student internship program between HSHMC and a neighborhood preK–6 school with a 95 percent population of English learners.

She earned a doctorate from Indiana University, a master's degree from Western Michigan University, and a bachelor's degree from Ohio Northern University.

To book Douglas Fisher, Nancy Frey, or Diane Lapp for professional development, contact pd@solution-tree.com. Douglas Fisher's Twitter feed is @dfishersdsu, and Nancy Frey's is @nancyfrey.

INTRODUCTION

Comprehension Occurs Through Text-Based Analysis and Discussion

WITHOUT QUESTION, INFORMATION IS more accessible today than ever before. Digital sources make it possible to locate anything from the works of Shakespeare to those of Stephenie Meyer within minutes. And despite the grave pronouncements of the death of the newspaper, we see people voraciously consuming up-to-the-minute news and information through a variety of electronic devices.

But access to information in the absence of critical thought is a dangerous recipe. No one would allow an untrained driver behind the steering wheel of a race car, yet we regularly put information in front of children and adolescents with little regard for how they will question, discuss, and formulate learned opinions about it. We leave students to superficially extract information about the text and then move almost immediately to their own connections. During class discussions, consumed by connections to their personal experiences, students veer off to the more interesting topic of another student's story, never to return to the text that started it all. Fourth-graders leave *Love That Dog* (Creech, 2001) to talk about their own loss of a beloved pet but don't discuss the poem "Love That Boy," by Walter Dean Myers, which is foundational to the book. Eleventh-graders read *The Grapes of Wrath* (Steinbeck, 1939/1992) and talk about the time they saw the film version but fail to recognize the author's socio-political viewpoint. Observing a student talking about a text is akin to watching an untrained driver swerve across three lanes to take the first exit she sees, never to return to the freeway that leads to her destination.

Perhaps missing a major theme in a book about a dead dog doesn't seem all that dangerous. But as educators in a world driven by a 24/7 news cycle, we are alarmed by the compartmentalization of information in our society. Increasingly, the public consumes news selectively, based on a set of preconceived assumptions. It is becoming rarer to hear and discuss opposing viewpoints. In addition, information consumption is changing the level of responsibility one has for making informed decisions. According to Tom Rosenstiel (2008), director of the Pew Research Center's Project for Excellence in Journalism:

> People are becoming their own editors, checking for news throughout the day, hunting through links and aggregators to find what they want, sorting among many sources, while also looking for overviews of what's new today—and sharing what they find with friends. In short, news consumption is shifting from being a passive act—tell me a story—to a proactive one—answer my question.

The habits of asking questions, discussing concepts, and formulating opinions are vital in an age when we are becoming our own editors. To teach reading and writing as a passive act when, in fact, it has become far more proactive leaves our learners vulnerable to propaganda, half-truths, and one-sided opinions. Hate speech on a website, a posted video rant about an individual, the whispered gossip about a classmate that is spread through instant messaging—all are fueled by consumers who fail to interrogate the text, who fail to analyze text messages, both those that are easy to identify and those that can only be identified by digging deep to glean how the reader is being positioned to think and believe. Students must be taught to analyze a text with the eyes of a detective who is never content with surface-level impressions but instead continually returns to the text to consider information from many perspectives. This investigation is meant to assess and compare information from personal experiences and contrasting information sources, to expand and refine one's insights, to communicate, collaborate, and finally to offer fresh or expanded positions.

New technologies increase readers' abilities to scrutinize text with ever-expanding opportunities to obtain, understand, and express information. This is not a new phenomenon; throughout history, new literacy demands have emerged in response to social and technological changes. A society's or community's expectations of literacy continue to shift the actions of its participants. We propose that within classroom communities an instructional shift must occur that prepares students to investigate texts in ways that enable them to scrutinize, critically analyze, produce, and communicate information.

The Community Defines Literacy

How a community defines *literacy* profoundly influences the learning experiences of students in that community. Myers (1996) describes five types of literacy that have been recognized and valued at different periods in American history since colonial times: signature literacy, recording literacy, recitational literacy, analytic literacy, and now critical literacy. Before the founding of the United States, literacy was defined as the ability to write one's name. Literacy instruction then was fairly basic, and school time (when it was available) was typically devoted to other things, such as ensuring the moral and religious development of the young students. As public schooling became available in the early part of the 19th century, the ability to record (copy) texts grew in value. People struck out to establish new towns across an expanding land, and it was often necessary to record important documents for use in these communities.

The post–Civil War years ushered in a new wave of movement and migration that was hastened by the Industrial Revolution. Single males led this migration. When many of them later settled and started families, their children needed an education that moved beyond the signature and recording literacies of previous generations. Newer beliefs about the role of school as a venue for teaching moral and civic ideology emerged. Schooling practices again shifted to reflect community definitions of literacy, and classrooms from 1864 to 1916 were filled with children reciting long memorized passages from works of literature, religious works, and civic documents—proof of being an educated person (Myers, 1996). Few schoolchildren of this period could exit school without being able to recite passages from Longfellow's "Song of Hiawatha," the Ten Commandments, and the Declaration of Independence.

Myers cites the 1894 work of the National Education Association's Committee of Ten as another important turning point in the evolution of literacy. The committee recommended that students receive eight years of elementary education and another four of high school. The group also determined that English should be considered a core subject, shepherding in another shift in curriculum and classroom instruction. (Fun fact: the Committee of Ten also recommended that science be taught in an alphabetical sequence—biology, chemistry, and physics—because the group couldn't agree on a conceptual progression.)

Myers (1996) states that with the introduction of longer works of literature, classroom reading went silent and recitation faded, and an analytic approach to literacy emerged. However, silent reading required other assessment measures, and the period from 1916 to 1983 saw a rise in a variety of testing approaches that required students to analyze texts in order to demonstrate their understanding. Teaching became "a bits-and-pieces interrogation of the student's mind . . . by a questioning system in which the teacher attempted to discover orally or in writing the various parts" of student understanding (p. 87). Coupled with such assessment came a new industry—textbooks—to further standardize curriculum. Over time, a new community of educational researchers emerged, becoming the arbiters of learnedness. This development reflected a growing demand in society at large for specialists who could fulfill specific functions.

But Myers (1996) notes that while some educators were defining literacy as a sum of parts, others were broadening the lens. A host of educators cautioned against the dangers of consuming information in an unquestioning way, warning that it would lead to a citizenry vulnerable to misinformation. Instead, they called for a new definition of literacy, one in which questioning, challenging, and consideration of multiple perspectives were vital. This approach, called *critical literacy*, involves acquiring and communicating information in ways that demonstrate an understanding of the social, political, and cultural contexts of an event. These analytic behaviors become possible as students are taught to read and think like detectives able to analyze, interrogate, and propose counterpositions to well-established institutional perspectives.

Today, we think about literacy in terms of the service role it plays in thinking and critical understanding. We focus on literacy because it is an access skill to understanding, not an end unto itself. In a 21st century classroom, students use their literacy skills in learning about and understanding the world around them. As the Common Core State Standards note, literacy is part of history, social sciences, science, and a wide range of technical fields.

The Common Core State Standards

Without question, the Common Core State Standards will have a profound influence on the education of students in the second decade of the 21st century. Developed by a consortium of educators and professionals through the facilitated efforts of the National Governors Association Center for Best Practices and the Council of Chief State School Officers, these standards are designed to align K–12 learning with college- and career-ready skills for a global economy. Consider the following sampling of standards in middle and high school English language arts (Common Core State Standards Initiative, 2010):

- Come to discussions prepared, having read or studied required material; explicitly draw on that preparation by referring to evidence on the topic, text, or issue to probe and reflect on ideas under discussion (Speaking & Listening, Grade 6, S.L.6.1).

- Present claims and findings, emphasizing salient points in a focused, coherent manner with relevant evidence, sound valid reasoning, and well-chosen details (Speaking & Listening, Grade 8, S.L.8.4).

- Determine an author's point of view or purpose in a text and analyze how an author uses rhetoric to advance that point of view or purpose (Reading: Informational Text, Grade 9–10, R.I.9-10.6).

- Gather relevant information from multiple authoritative print and digital sources, using advanced searches effectively; assess the strengths and limitations of each source in terms of the task, purpose, and audience (Writing, Grade 11-12, W.11-12.8).

The expectation that adolescents will be able to speak, listen, read, and write rhetorically shouldn't be too surprising. But now consider the following sampling of elementary school standards (Common Core State Standards Initiative, 2010):

- With prompting and support, identify the reasons an author gives to support points in a text (Reading: Informational Text, Kindergarten, RI.K.8).

- Build on others' talk in conversations by responding to the comments of others through multiple exchanges (Speaking and Listening, Grade 1, SL.1.1).

- Write opinion pieces in which they introduce the topic or book they are writing about, state an opinion, supply reasons that support the opinion, use linking words (e.g., *because, and, also*) to connect opinion and reasons, and provide a concluding statement or section (Writing, Grade 2, W.2.1).

- Refer to parts of stories, dramas, and poems when writing or speaking about a text, using terms such as chapter, scene, and stanza; describe how each successive part builds on earlier sections (Reading: Literature, Grade 3, RL.3.5).

- Acquire and use accurately grade-appropriate general academic and domain-specific words and phrases, including those that signal precise actions, emotions, or states of being (e.g., *quizzed, whined, stammered*) and that are basic to a particular topic (e.g., *wildlife, conservation*, and *endangered* when discussing animal preservation) (Language, Grade 4, L.4.6).

- Quote accurately from a text when explaining what the text says explicitly and when drawing inferences from the text (Reading: Informational Text, Grace 5, RI.5.1).

For many elementary educators, the degree of emphasis on such concepts is new territory. In our efforts to keep a necessary focus on developmental reading, the content of the materials has at times taken a backseat. However, the advent of more informational texts in the earliest grades has prompted a movement toward teaching students about the content itself (Duke, 2010). In other words, text-based discussions are not for secondary students alone. There is a growing appreciation of the fact that students must be taught, from the time they first learn to read—that the text itself is of importance and is not merely a springboard for other topics.

We have seen this orientation back to the text in the practices of teachers who discuss the author's craft with their students, noting how passages are carefully written to carry a story. Young children engage in text-based discussions when they compare the works of an author/illustrator such as Eric Carle. Importantly, they involve themselves in text-based discussions when they pore over the photographic illustrations in a science book, debating the details they see in the picture. Unfortunately, these episodes are rare in some classrooms, and the discussion is dominated instead by personal anecdotes that have limited value beyond eliciting a passing interest. The habit of close reading as a means for supporting discussion about the text doesn't simply develop—it must be purposefully taught, beginning in the first years of school.

Discussing Worthy Texts

Standards such as the ones quoted previously are designed to encourage close reading and discussion of worthy texts. As Newkirk (2010) notes in his article "The Case for Slow Reading," not all texts demand such attention. But it is vital to recognize that more complex texts require the reader to return to them, as "we never really 'comprehend' these anchoring passages—we're never done with them; we never consume them. Like sacred texts, they are inexhaustible, continuing to move us, support us, and even surprise us" (p. 11). Perhaps an incidental benefit of an approach that demands close reading and discussion is that it affords students a luxury we have taken for granted as teachers. Each year, we read, discuss, and write about the texts we use in our classrooms. We rarely read something once and then teach it, never to return to it again. And each time we do so, we discover a new insight between the lines of the text.

Although we will leave to others the debate about what constitutes a "worthy text," we agree that the issue of text complexity, featured prominently in the Common Core State Standards, is an important one. Published examples of what is identified as grade- or course-appropriate complex text may give many educators pause. How can students who are reading well below grade level read and understand these texts? The answer, we believe, lies in reading shorter pieces of complex text repeatedly and discussing what the text contains. While a longer reading may in fact be too difficult for a struggling reader, a shorter one, read several times as part of the discourse about the piece, increases the reader's ability to understand the text. The staircase effect, meant to advance readers across a range of literature and informational texts, occurs as students engage in discussion of what the text does and does not offer. In turn, students are encouraged to locate further information or perspectives that illuminate the topic. Perhaps David Coleman (2010), project editor for the Common Core English language arts standards said it best: "We want students to read like detectives and write like reporters."

What Is Text-Based Discussion?

A text-based-discussion approach challenges students to extract information from the text, consider their own experiences and background knowledge, and engage in academic talk about ideas and concepts. But it doesn't stop there. This approach demands that students read, write, and think rhetorically in order to interrogate the text itself: Where did this come from? What influenced its creation? How does the author's viewpoint shape this text? What other perspectives need to be explored? What might be missing? By posing and exploring these questions in depth, with the text itself at the center, students become more sophisticated readers, writers, and thinkers.

Text-based discussions are fostered by the purposeful instructional moves of the teacher. By modeling the ways in which we interpret, reread, and consult the text, we demonstrate habits of mind for our students. Guided instruction allows us to observe the extent to which our students are using these critical thinking skills and helps us determine what we need to teach next. Productive group work provides a format for small groups of students to delve deeply into text to consolidate their understanding of it, preparing them for the independent learning of a reader who approaches text as a resource for understanding the world (Fisher & Frey, 2008b).

What You Can Expect From This Book

The subsequent chapters of this book explore the relationship between text, learner, and learning as students engage in discussion and rhetorical reading and writing in elementary, middle, and high school settings. We agree with Britton (1983), who stated, "Writing floats on a sea of talk" (p. 11). We would further argue that reading does, too. Therefore, chapter 1 is dedicated to principles of discussion and discourse that lead to deep learning. Chapter 2 explains principles of argumentation and rhetoric, which are common in high school English classrooms but less widely known in other grade levels and content areas.

The next chapters address how to use discourse and rhetoric in conjunction with narrative and informational texts. We are especially concerned that narrative texts not be excluded from this practice, particularly because they hold such rich promise for deep discussion. Thus chapter 3 offers examples of text-based discussions about fiction. Informational texts are used at the secondary level in great numbers and across all the content areas. In chapter 4, we describe how teachers can use the features and structures of these texts to foster student thinking. Finally, in chapter 5, we build on the previous chapters to discuss how new media influence the ways both narrative and informational texts are located, shared, and created.

Because discussion is the centerpiece for this book, you will find extended student dialogue throughout. We invite you to do your own slow reading of these passages. As professionals, we understand the need to skim reading material to get the gist of a concept. However, we selected these dialogues not only to illustrate but also to expand on the ideas in the main portions of the text. As you read these passages, listen for the ways students build their understanding of ideas, sometimes in fits and starts. And then try your hand at engaging in the practices we're advocating in this book.

CHAPTER 1

Readers and Texts: Why Both Are Necessary for Understanding

"ONE TIME, AT BAND CAMP . . ." You know where this is going. The student is going to make a tangentially related connection between himself and the text, based on a personal experience that few, if any, other students have had. Although the student has comprehended the gist of what the author has shared, this personal connection may overshadow the message of the text and move him further and further away from the text and what the author had to say. When this happens, reading becomes primarily about the reader's experience and not about maintaining a relationship between the text and the reader, who as a result may fail to comprehend the complexity of the information being presented.

But making the personal connection is not the problem. In fact, making connections is what readers often do when comprehending and enjoying a text. As we will see later in this chapter, making connections is one of the cognitive strategies readers use to understand what they are reading. The problem is that less-able readers do not return to the text to compare and contrast their personal experience with that of the author (Cordón & Day, 1996). Either they have not been taught the reasons for returning to the text or they have not been held accountable for applying them.

Before continuing, we want to clarify that we use the term *text* with an expanded definition that includes newspapers, photographs, video clips, poems, and any other sources of information that a teacher can use to center classroom conversation.

Proficient readers actively and reciprocally draw on their experiences to compare, contrast, validate, and extend what they are reading (Pressley, 2000). For example, consider the discussion a group of students had while reading *The Absolutely True Diary of a Part-Time Indian* (Alexie, 2007), a book that recounts the trials of a Native

American teenager, nicknamed Junior, who chooses to attend a "white" school rather than the school on his reservation.

> **BRIAN:** I think it's good how this chapter started about Thanksgiving. I could really see this in my mind.
>
> **ANDREA:** Yeah, cuz it's something we all do every year. We all have turkey and a big dinner at Thanksgiving.
>
> **BRIAN:** And all those other things, like pumpkin pie and cranberry sauce. We never eat those, except for Thanksgiving. I don't know why.
>
> **SPENSER:** And Junior doesn't know why they eat this stuff either.
>
> **ANDREA:** Yeah, because, like he says, the Indians and Pilgrims were best friends at first, and then the Pilgrims started shooting Indians.
>
> **BRIAN:** That's another reason some of his friends don't like that he goes to the white school.
>
> **ANDREA:** Like Rowdy, who pretends not to be home when Junior goes to his house on Thanksgiving?
>
> **BRIAN:** Even when he drew that cartoon of them back when they were friends.
>
> **ANDREA:** It doesn't seem like a very good Thanksgiving. He still doesn't have his best friend, and he's eating the same food as white people.
>
> **BRIAN:** I can see why he asks what there is to be thankful for.
>
> **SPENSER:** His dad says that they should be thankful because every Indian wasn't killed.

Throughout this discussion, these students related what they were reading to their prior experiences. But unlike the student who makes a personal connection and leaves the text behind, these students returned to the text to support and extend their ideas and claims.

This type of conversation is not limited to adolescents who have extensive experience with texts. We've seen kindergarten classrooms in which students regularly return to the text in their discussions. For example, a group of students were discussing the poem "Be Glad Your Nose Is on Your Face" (Prelutsky, 1999). The teacher had read the entire poem aloud once and then had reread the poem, pausing this time to think aloud about the meaning of some of the words, such as *precious, dread*, and *despair*. On her third reading of the poem, the students engaged in partner talk about each stanza and then discussed with the whole class what they thought about the poem. At one point, Amir announced that he wouldn't like his nose to be between his toes—based on the fact that his father's feet smelled. Several other students r their hands with stories about family members with smelly feet. Maria returned th conversation to the text saying, "I get it. It says that it 'would not be a treat,' so it's not fun to have to smell feet all of the time." Khalid agreed, saying, "Oh, like the picture right here" (pointing to the illustration). "That would be only what you smell. Not like putting your nose there, but your nose is there all the time."

As with the adolescents reading Sherman Alexie's (2007) book, these kindergartners comprehended more when they regularly returned to the text to compare their perspective with the author's words. In doing so, they learned to interact with the text. Importantly, they also learned to interact with one another. We'll take up both kinds of interaction next.

Interacting With Texts

All readers interact with texts. Interacting with texts does not mean that readers have to agree with everything they read. Our point is not to suggest that reading instruction focus on determining the author's point and analyzing only the author's message. In other words, we're not suggesting a return to New Critical theory (for example, Welleck & Warren, 1949), which focused instruction on the accurate and "correct" interpretation of the text, often through an analysis of the narrator and the point of view. As Langer (1994) points out, the New Critical–theory approach is text based and assumes that meaning resides within the text. According to this tradition, students are taught to analyze the text for its inherent meaning and are expected to put aside their own experiences and perspectives.

Interestingly, New Critical theory sought to eliminate discussions about the author's biography or the social and historical context in which the text was written. The idea was that readers should attend to the formal features of the text and should base their analyses only on the observable features of that specific piece of work. Frankly, this idea is old-fashioned and inconsistent with the demands of reading, not to mention the focus of the Common Core State Standards, which require that students consider the sociopolitical and historical context of the text. Just imagine a reader reading *The Grapes of Wrath* (Steinbeck, 1939/1992) without considering the history of the Great Depression or the experiences of migrant farm workers. The reader can still understand the book, but the experience will be different compared with that of a reader who integrates his or her knowledge of these historical times and human experiences.

The theory that replaced New Critical theory focuses on reader response (for example, Iser, 1978; Tompkins, 1980). While reader response theory is still not totally accepted, there is growing recognition that the reader brings understandings and experiences to the text that are used to make meaning. As Sheridan Blau (1994) suggests, "A work of literature is an inert text that can hardly be said to have more than a potential for meaning until it is called into being by a reader who constructs a

ving meaning to the text" (p. 26). Louise Rosenblatt (1978) notes,
nts of the work—style and structure, rhythmic flow—function
total literary experience" (p. 7).

eader response theory, there are as many interpretations of a given
eaders. This is, in part, why readers like—and need—to talk with
t they are reading. Readers' experiences, or biases, are determined
by their own race, gender, socioeconomic status, background experiences, academic
history, geography, and so on. Readers who share any of these perspectives often
have similar reactions to a text. For example, *The Skin I'm In* (Flake, 1998) resonated
with our African American students, who had a shared experience with the author.
During a class discussion, Shannon noted that she was the same color as the character, "a warm cup of cocoa" (p. 41), and talked about how that made her feel. The other
students weren't really into the book until they considered the perspectives of their
peers. By the end of the book, every student had a deepened understanding of the
text. As Luz, an immigrant from Mexico said, "Maleeka [the main character] helped
me love my skin, too. She didn't put up with racism or even hate from her own race.
When you love the skin you're in, you get a better life 'cause you're not spending too
much time worried about what people are thinking."

We'll focus on the importance of discussion in the next section. Before we do
so, we need to look more closely at reader response theory. In the writings of some
reader response theorists, the balance between the reader and the text has tipped
totally to the reader. This view is really no better than that of New Critical theory,
in which the reader was forgotten and the entire focus was on the text. Some reader
response theorists rationalize the exclusive focus on the reader as the implementation
of Louise Rosenblatt's ideas. But Rosenblatt (1995) does not focus exclusively on the
reader; rather, she focuses on the transaction between the reader and the text. In her
words, "The reader must remain faithful to the author's text and must be alert to the
potential clues concerning character and motive" (p. 11). Rosenblatt cautions that
readers might ignore elements in a text and fail to realize that they are "imputing to
the author views unjustified by the text" (p. 11).

Part of Rosenblatt's work focuses on the various ways that readers approach the
text. She suggests that these ways include efferent or aesthetic responses, described
as follows:

- **Efferent reading.** In this type of reading, the reader wants to "take away"
particular bits of information. It's a more public form of reading, meaning
that the reader pays attention to facts, concepts, and solutions that can be
taken away from the reading. Rosenblatt (1978) states, "The reader's attention
is primarily focused on what will remain as a residue after the reading—the
information to be acquired, the logical solution to a problem, the actions to be
carried out" (p. 23). An example would be reading a technical manual about

sailing or reading a textbook to learn about advances in navigation between World Wars I and II.

- **Aesthetic reading**. In this type of reading, the reader wants to explore the work and oneself. This method is a more private form of reading, meaning that the reader pays attention to emotions, feelings, attitudes, and ideas: "In aesthetic reading, the reader's attention is centered directly on what he is living through during his relationship with that particular text" (Rosenblatt, 1978, p. 25). An example would be reading *Moby-Dick* (Melville, 1851/1963) to vicariously live through a sailing adventure. One would not read *Moby-Dick* to learn how to sail or to learn about advances in navigation.

Importantly, both efferent and aesthetic responses are necessary for readers to fully experience the text. In fact, Rosenblatt (1995) thought of them as two ends of a continuum in which the reader "focuses attention on the stream of consciousness, selecting out the particular mix of public and private linkages with the words dictated by the purpose of the reading" (p. 293). As we will explore in greater detail in subsequent chapters of this book, students need to return to the text and make connections with their own relevantly related experiences (Williams, 1993). As readers develop this skill, they realize that making these connections is where comprehension begins, not ends. To become proficient with this approach, students need to talk about the texts they are reading and be supported as they experiment with this interactive, text-and-talk process.

Consider the discussion a group of third-graders had about *Charlotte's Web* (White, 1952). The majority of their discussion fell on the aesthetic end of the continuum, as they worried about Wilbur's fate and laughed at Templeton's actions. But their interaction with the text was not exclusively aesthetic. The students regularly included more efferent comments as they learned about barns and other factual information from the book. Interestingly, when Charlotte described making a web, the students' reading moved significantly into the efferent domain, and they learned scientific information that they could take away. Zach even went to the library to find more books about spider-web design so that he could validate and extend the knowledge he gained from Charlotte's explanation. As Zach later told his group, "Spiders don't really fly from one side to the other side. They let the wind blow them to the other side. When they get to the right place, they make the attachment and then go back along that line to make it stronger. Sometimes, they have to wait a long time for the right place to make the first thread."

While the teacher's original purpose was not efferent—she didn't focus the class on spider-web design—the class moved in that direction as part of their natural reading. Because their teacher allowed space for them to blend their efferent and aesthetic interpretations, the students also made a number of aesthetic connections, such as Edgar's comment, "I kinda cried when Charlotte died. It made me think of my grandma. But I was happy again, when I figured out that there were a whole bunch of little Charlottes born that would start all over again. Wilbur is lucky."

The balance of aesthetic and efferent responses is not limited to children's literature. It's how we all read. We move along the continuum based on the purpose for our reading and the things that happen in our minds as we read. For example, in another classroom as sixteen-year-old Taryn read *The Metamorphosis* (Kafka, 1946) on her iPad, she moved back and forth on the continuum between efferent responses and aesthetic responses. At one point, she said, "His mom wanted to go in and see him, but his dad and sister wouldn't let her go in. I guess that's because he looks too gross and that they would be afraid. But they let him live there. They must know that the 'vermin,' as it said back on page one, is their son, at least on some level." At another point, she said, "I don't get the sick-day policy. My boss wouldn't show up at my house if I missed one day of work. It must have been different in that time. Maybe they didn't have benefits or something. Does anyone know?"

As we saw with the third-graders, Taryn's reading purpose also changed based on what she was reading at the moment. She adjusted her response and brought her experiences to bear on the text. And that is what this book is about: teaching students to return to the text in their discussions. Students will expand their understanding of what they read when they integrate their own responses with what the author offers, taking into account the sociopolitical and historical context of the text. Of course, every reader doesn't have the same background knowledge, so a further benefit of reading and then engaging in discussions with others is that students can also expand their knowledge base.

Comprehending, Analyzing, and Discussing Texts

The language of text manifests itself in the spoken language of students engaged in discussion. Most reading instruction includes multiple forms of discussion as students talk about what they have read, their responses to it, and an evaluation of it. Text-based discussions often occur in small groups, such as in literature circles, so that all students can participate (Daniels, 2002). A number of researchers (for example, Clarke, Snowling, Truelove, & Hulme, 2010; Tharp & Gallimore, 1988; Wells & Wells, 1989) have examined the phenomenon of realization of ideas through discussion, as when Marta, a student of ours, remarked, "I didn't know what I thought about the story until I started talking about it!" For emergent readers, text-based discussions lead to the realization that "reading is not just recognizing and saying the words" (Blum, Koskinen, Bhartiya, & Hluboky, 2010, p. 495).

While most teachers claim that they want to foster discussion in the classroom, in practice they may be reluctant to give up their traditional attitudes about the roles of teachers and students. A classroom that supports discussion requires that teachers adopt two fundamental values. The first is acknowledging that students have something worthwhile to say and that students' views may differ from what the teacher believes. The second is accepting that teachers will have to relinquish some of the "teacher as the only source of information" control.

Acknowledging That Students Have Something to Say

Not long ago, Nancy facilitated a graduate-course discussion based on the question, "Does disability exist?" The students had read several short stories and research articles about perceptions of ability and disability and had participated in text-based discussions about each one. On this evening, students formed groups of five to explore questions around the topic and synthesize across texts. Although many of the articles forwarded beliefs about disability as a manmade construct rather than a natural part of the human condition, one student, Felice, stood firm in her belief that disability is concrete and quantifiable. She crossed her arms, leaned back in her chair, and said, "I've got a sibling who's never going to talk. No matter what anyone says, he has a disability. Period."

Nancy had a dilemma on her hands: should she express her own opinion, which would likely overpower the group, or allow the discussion to follow its course? "Can you say some more about that?" she asked. "I sense that you're feeling frustrated by the conversation, and it sounds like we need to hear what you have to say."

For the next few minutes, Felice shared her personal experiences of growing up with a sibling who does not communicate using spoken language. These experiences shaped her view, and without an opportunity to express them safely, she was immune to other viewpoints. Her fellow students took her perspectives into account as the discussion continued. "I'm really moved by what Felice has told us," offered one group member. "It makes me think of what the author says about wearing a T-shirt that read, 'Not being able to speak isn't the same as not having something to say.'" Turning to Felice, the student said, "Maybe you don't disagree with the author as much as you thought you did."

Nancy was impressed with the way the group listened carefully and integrated Felice's experiences into the discussion. In addition, the group steered itself back to the texts. Personal connections matter in a text-based discussion, but they are risky, especially when a student's experiences differ from those of the teacher. Nancy could easily have negated Felice's experience with a barrage of research and published opinions, but it would have benefited neither Felice nor the rest of the group. Instead, the students acknowledged that one level of understanding the text stems from personal experience, which in turn can enhance other students' understanding. But without a return to the text itself, there was a risk that the discussion would move further away from the purpose of the discussion itself.

Students arrive in our classrooms with viewpoints shaped by their backgrounds and experiences, which are sometimes very different from those of the teacher. As educators, we must not advance an additional bias toward the "right" answer. Just as New Critical theory narrowed the reader's understanding of the text, so can the teacher's viewpoints be used to constrain conversation. No one should be allowed to engage in hateful or hurtful comments that alienate the people inside the classroom or out. But a disapproving look, a limp comment ("That's nice. Anyone else?"), or a quick retort can end a line of discourse before it's ever had a chance to bloom.

We've seen this shutdown happen during brainstorming. The leader poses a question, takes five responses that are usually pretty conventional, gets the answer he wants, and then moves on. No more brainstorming! A similar phenomenon can take place in text-based discussions, especially when a student offers a perspective that is different from the teacher's or when a student who is intent on proving his or her point offers a position with such emphatic intent that other perspectives are silenced.

Fourth-grade teacher Rebecca Clark faced this situation when a group of her students were discussing a late chapter from the book *From the Mixed-Up Files of Mrs. Basil E. Frankweiler* (Konigsberg, 1967). Although Claudia, the protagonist, had agreed to keep a secret about a Michelangelo sculpture because it made her feel special, one of the students, Ben, had a different opinion of why she acted as she did. "I think she liked the idea of not having to share something. She was always selfish," he stated. While Ms. Clark didn't share Ben's opinion of the main character, she was interested in his take on this. "That's an interesting idea. What's your evidence for that, Ben? Be sure to use the book," she added.

Ben immediately turned to the first chapter. "Claudia said she chose to run away with her second brother because he was rich," he said, pointing to the sentence. "Not so much because she liked him, but because he would have money because he saved his allowance. Not like her." Ms. Clark and the other students debated for several minutes whether Claudia was indeed selfish, and then the teacher invited the students to look back in the text for evidence of Claudia's generosity or selfishness. Gradually, the group reached general consensus that Claudia was more self-centered than selfish. The fact that Ms. Clark used restraint in responding to Ben led to a rich discussion about the main character and her actions.

Relinquishing Some Control of the Discourse

Teachers actually use discussions more rarely than they report that they do (Nystrand, 1997). Inexperienced teachers have greater difficulty posing questions that require discussion. A study of the questioning habits of novice and experienced (more than four years) teachers found that only 15 percent of the questions inexperienced teachers asked invited discussion, compared to 32 percent in the more experienced group (Tienken, Goldberg, & DiRocco, 2009). Many beginning teachers we know have shared that although they love to have students converse, they never know how to get the conversation recentered on the text. Their reluctance to engage in extended discussions with students is often due to issues about classroom control and loss of instructional focus. Classroom management is a real consideration, and we do not advocate for an anything-goes environment, in which students talk over one another. Expectations about active listening and turn taking should be taught and revisited throughout the school year. The other concern, that extended discussion can lead the group too far away from the intended focus, is also a very real problem. In fact, it is the basis for this book. We find that the way to avoid tangential discussions is to return the conversation to the text.

Many teachers report that students are reluctant to participate in extended discussions. The classroom environment can greatly influence students' willingness to participate. A number of conditions must be present for students to feel comfortable enough to contribute to discussions. First among them is that discussions occur regularly and throughout the day. We've witnessed the startled looks of students who are unexpectedly roused to discuss something after an extended teacher monologue. The second condition that must be present is a sense of psychological safety. Having clear norms and rules contributes to this feeling, as does the teacher's maintaining an appropriate level of control.

Hadjioannou (2007) studied a fifth-grade classroom in which text-based discussions occurred frequently to glean what environmental factors contributed to student participation and rich discourse. She identified five conditions:

1. A standing invitation for participation

2. Encouragement to listen attentively and build on the ideas of others

3. The right to raise issues and influence the direction of the discussion

4. An expectation that students would express opinions

5. The use of textual evidence to support ideas

These conditions certainly promote a conversational model that differs from the traditional classroom discourse pattern of initiate, respond, evaluate (IRE) that Cazden (2001) describes. Usually, the teacher *initiates* conversation by posing a question or making a statement that invites student *response*. After the student offers a response, the teacher *evaluates* its correctness and then, if the response is correct, continues with this pattern of interrogation. If the response is not the one the teacher anticipated, he or she calls on another student to offer the correct response. Since most of us have been engaged in classroom IRE interactions, it is easy to see that this type of instruction parallels a model of recitation rather than conversation because the teacher has a set answer in mind and has only prompted the student to supply it. Mehan (1979) describes these questions as pseudoquestions that teachers ask to quiz students rather than to truly engage them in conversation.

We are proposing a very different model of conversation. As illustrated in the following exchange among third-graders who were reading *Gold Fever! Tales From the California Gold Rush* by Rosalyn Schanzer (2007), which was one text source in their study of the California Gold Rush, we are encouraging inquiry as students discover and expand on information gleaned from ideas that are text based and peer shared.

NICK:	The quote by Sarah Royce says that she sees a mirage that was a small lake. Then it says as she got closer it disappeared. How could that happen? Was she cuckoo?
ALLY:	No, she just thought she saw it because she was so thirsty, and she was hoping it was there.
NICK:	How could anybody be that thirsty?
DAVE:	My dad said that when he was in the army, he got separated from his buddies, and as he wandered around the desert he thought he saw a lake. He told me that he was so thirsty and the sun was playing tricks on his eyes that made the sand look like water. He thought he was going to die if he didn't reach the water.
MIKE:	Wow, what happened to him?
DAVE:	He was spotted by other army guys in a helicopter.
MS. JACKSON:	(connecting the conversation and the text) What happened to your dad and also to Sarah Royce is that they became delusional because of a lack of water and also because of the way the light was hitting the ground.
KATIE:	Does *delusional* mean you think something is real when it isn't?
DAVE:	Yeah, I remember my dad said he was delusional.
NICK:	Okay, so even though they both knew there isn't water in the desert, because of the weird light and how thirsty they were, they thought they saw water. Wow—intense!
ALLY:	Yeah, and Sarah knew she only had a little water left.
MS. JACKSON:	Terrific thinking. Can someone share the words in the text that show us Sarah's thinking?

As the children and Ms. Jackson continue this conversation, the teacher encourages her students by probing, clarifying, and offering cues that illustrate how to use one's related knowledge and text information to deeply comprehend the author's message. This interaction illustrates peer discussion as a delineated segment of intentional instruction. Referred to by Applebee, Langer, Nystrand, and Gamoran (2003) as *open or free discussion*, intentional discussion occurs among a small group of students for approximately thirty seconds. During this time, students must be free to share and explore information that in some way relates to the target concept. As they listen to and interact with peers, they are able to expand their understanding of the target and related concepts. As you saw, Ms. Jackson expertly used Ally's comment to invite students to again connect to the text. As teachers model reconnecting with the text to validate and extend conversation, they illustrate for students the interactive play between the reader and the author.

Balancing Discussion and Instruction

Langer (1985, 1987) invites educators to consider a sociocognitive perspective as a way to support the relationship between language and literacy. She highlights how the context of the classroom promotes particular ways of thinking and acting. The context created in a given classroom can foster interaction, discussion, and the use of evidence in argumentation. Understanding the sociocultural context and working to create a classroom that encourages thinking promotes better teaching and learning. As she and others (Alvermann et al., 1996; Eeds & Wells, 1989; Johnston, 2004) have noted, teachers should view the exchange of information through a discussion of ideas as a foundational element for classroom literacy teaching and learning. When teachers develop this perspective, the goal of their instruction changes from presenting content and building consensus to availing students of multiple opportunities to interact with peers and text while examining many perspectives (Langer, 1995). Text-based conversations encourage the voicing of understandings and misunderstandings, thereby enriching students' cognitive and linguistic repertoires. Through these conversations, students develop knowledge and skills that support their expanding comprehension and strengthen their beliefs in their abilities to contribute and succeed.

Scaffolding Text-Based Analysis and Discussion

In *Reading to Learn: Lessons From Exemplary Fourth-Grade Teachers*, Allington and Johnston (2002) invite readers to visit classrooms where extremely effective teachers promote *tentative talk*, which the authors describe as open-ended exchanges among students that allow them to build from one another's thoughts as they talk about text-related ideas. If you have ever tried to promote such discussions in your classroom, you know that they do not just happen. They are instead the result of careful planning, continuous evaluation, modeling, and much supported scaffolding that moves students from uncertainty about how to engage in conversation to the "grand conversations" described by Eeds and Wells (1989).

Scaffolded text-based discussions offer students the information they need in order to have a free-flowing conversation that meanders to and from the information shared in the text. In the previous example of Ms. Jackson and a group of students talking about the water mirage, the teacher entered the conversation only to model for her students how to contrast their thinking with the information shared in the text. As students become able to seamlessly make these connections, the teacher offers fewer instructional scaffolds. You cannot be part of every discussion that occurs in the classroom, but when you do participate, you can model the scaffolds needed to help students know how to conduct high-quality, text-related conversational exchanges. They will learn that these exchanges result from participating and being engaged, expanding and wondering about text and peer statements, offering examples that help with clarification, promoting discussion through questioning and elaborating, and using the text and related experiences for validation, illumination, and reference. You can scaffold a group discussion by interjecting statements and questions like these:

- Tell me in your own words what happened in the book.
- Talk about your favorite parts.
- This book reminds me of . . .
- Add something new to the book (Blum et al., 2010, p. 495).
- I think this means . . .
- I'm wondering if . . .
- Can you share more about . . . ?
- I don't understand the meaning of . . . Can someone help?
- That character reminds me of . . .
- If what you said is true, then why would . . . ?

Notice how each of these statements and questions is an attempt to promote text-related talk. For students to learn this skill, they must be given opportunities to practice and to watch exchanges being modeled by an expert or teacher. By talking with their teacher and peers about the texts they are reading, students will develop a fuller comprehension of the author's message as well as their own related positions.

Using Cognitive Strategies

The cognitive strategies readers use to understand texts have been the focus of much recent attention. These strategies include such mental moves as making connections, visualizing, questioning, predicting, inferring, synthesizing and summarizing, and monitoring. Importantly, each strategy requires that the reader return to the text to determine what the author has to offer. There must be a balance between the reader and the text, and leaning too much on one side or the other compromises or even prevents understanding. We'll consider each of the cognitive comprehension strategies in turn and look at how readers use the text when employing it. In reality, none of these strategies is used in isolation, but instead, depending on what comprehension needs are triggered by the text, a proficient reader draws from his or her bank of familiar strategies to support meaning making.

Making Connections

Text-to-self, text-to-text, and text-to-world connections are among the most common comprehension strategies taught, and they are also the ones that place the reader most at risk for leaving the text and going on a personal journey. That's not to say that readers should avoid making connections; they are important ways to make sense of what one is reading. They are also important for motivation, as readers need to see themselves in the texts they read. But readers also need to understand the point that the author is trying to make.

Sometimes the connections are obviously not helpful, as was the case when we observed a teacher introduce the fable "The Tortoise and the Hare." Jonathan couldn't wait to talk and share his text-to-self connection about the turtle he had at home, including a lengthy description of what it ate. In this case, the connection wasn't relevant to the reading. The fact that the turtle moved slowly might have been more relevant, but even that connection is less important than an understanding of fables and why we tell them.

Compare the turtle experience with the connection Alexis made while listening to her teacher read *Rose Blanche* (Innocenti, 1985): "This reminds me of that other book we read, like last week. I remember Nazis from *The Butterfly* [Polacco, 2000]. They were the soldiers for Hitler who took away people from their houses. They are drawn all scary with gray color in both books." This connection drove the reader back into the text to assess the relevance of the connection and her understanding of the text. Like other comprehension strategies, making connections is helpful when students return to the text for evidence or reference. Again, that's not to say that readers should simply analyze the text that the author presents, but they should not lose sight of the words on the page or screen as they make connections.

Visualizing

Creating visual images is another way that readers comprehend the texts they read. Like making connections, playing a movie in one's mind can lead a reader astray. The goal of visualizing is not to create your own film, but rather to see the images created with the words. Visualizing helps the reader fill in the missing parts and gain a deeper understanding of the text. Often, readers use visualizing with narrative texts or fiction. For example, when an author describes the setting, readers can visualize the scene. But visualizing is not limited to narrative texts; it can be used equally effectively with informational texts. For example, a group of students were reading *How Animals Shed Their Skin* (Tatham, 2002). In the following conversation, they not only make use of visualizing but also refer back to the text to aid their understanding:

GEORGE: I didn't know that frogs shed their skin. I can't really see that in my mind.

AMBER: But it does. See right here? It says, "Because a frog's skin can't grow, it must be shed" [p. 30].

MARICELLA: Don't picture a snake. It's different. For the frog, it splits open on the back and then the frog has to get out. Can you see that in your mind?

GEORGE: I guess. Like it splits back (pointing to a frog picture) here? I guess I can see that because the frog got too big for its skin and kinda popped out.

AMBER: Yeah, like that, but slower. It has to take some time to get out of the old skin.

MARICELLA: And this is cool. It eats the old skin in one piece. I can totally see that. It's kinda gross, but I can see the frog eating it and then jumping in the water again.

GEORGE: Yeah, cool, I can see that.

Questioning

Asking questions while reading is a natural habit most readers already possess. We internally argue and debate with the author and ask questions as we read. In doing so, we engage in a transaction between ourselves, as readers, and the text. But sometimes these questions take us away from the text. Of course, questions that drive readers to find out something new or pause and think about something are important. For example, while reading *If I Only Had a Horn: Young Louis Armstrong* (Orgill, 1997), Amanda wondered what the music sounded like. She stopped reading and Googled "Louis Armstrong songs." She found several on YouTube, including "What a Wonderful World." In Amanda's case, her questions led her to find out something new and interesting—but she never finished reading the text she had selected.

For Amanda, at this time and for this reading, it's probably not so important that she didn't finish the book. But sometimes it is important that students continue to read the text and ask questions along the way. In those cases, students must learn to ask questions of the author and return to the text to find answers. As we will discuss in greater detail in chapter 4, one of the ways to do this is through reciprocal teaching (Palincsar & Brown, 1984). Another way to do this is through discussions. When students ask and answer questions, they can learn to request evidence from the text they are reading. For example, while reading the short story "Salvador Late or Early" (Cisneros, 1991), one of the students asked, "Is Salvador happy?" A number of students responded, each with their evidence from the text:

BRANDI: No way. The teacher doesn't even know his name.

TIM: I agree. He's really poor and not happy. It says right here that he lives where the houses are the color of bad weather. That's all gray and stuff.

DESTINI: I think he is happy. He has one hundred balloons of happiness and one guitar for grief.

MICHAEL: But his mom trusts him with his brothers while she is busy with the baby. That's makes you proud, happy.

The conversation these students had suggests that they had read the text deeply. They didn't simply determine what the author said; they used their own perspectives and experiences. But they also provided evidence from the text for their responses. Their text-based discussion helped them reach a higher level of understanding, one informed by the reactions and perspectives of their peers.

Predicting

Making educated guesses about the text and what might come next is one way that readers remain engaged with their reading. Predicting is not a simple process of wild guessing. It requires that readers use what the author provides and integrate that with their background knowledge and experience.

Useful predictions allow the reader to analyze the text, taking into account his or her knowledge of the genre and the ways of the world. As we have noted, an understanding of the text read thus far is critical in forming a prediction. Of course, this cognitive comprehension strategy is often misused, as when the teacher holds up a book like *The Old Man and the Sea* (Hemingway, 1952/1996) and asks students to make a prediction about the content of the book. Yeah, an old man goes out to sea. What good did that prediction do for the reader? Instead, the key to predicting is to identify places in the text where making a prediction is helpful and then to revisit the prediction to determine if any clues were missed. When students say, "I totally missed that," we know that they are revisiting their predictions and considering what the text has to offer. We observed this happen when Jeff was reading *Harry Potter and the Prisoner of Azkaban* (Rowling, 1999). He said, "I should have known Professor Lupin was a werewolf. All the clues were there. Even his name, Lupin, is like lupus, the wolf."

Inferring

Authors do not tell their readers everything. Not only would that be boring, but also they'd run out of pages. Accordingly, inferring requires that students pay attention to the text. Reading between the lines is a complex skill that students develop with practice. Like predicting, inferring is not wild guessing. Inferences require a sophisticated understanding of the text combined with knowledge about the world.

As a fairly extreme example of inferring, in which readers must use clues the author provides in order to piece together meaning, read "Jabberwocky," by Lewis Carroll (1872/1996). The words are made up, but inferencing skills work. While they answer in the nonsense words the author provides, readers must also figure out what Carroll is trying to say. Students can easily answer the following questions by returning to the text:

- What did the toves do?
- What kind of sword did the son have?
- What were the borogoves?

Although "Jabberwocky" is fun and interesting to read, and provides students with an example of inferencing, the reality is that students have to learn to do this in all kinds of texts. For example, when the first-graders in Mr. Zemlick's class were reading *Click, Clack, Moo: Cows That Type* (Cronin, 2000), John inferred, "Those cows are typing again" when the teacher read the phrase "click, clack, moo." Later in the book, when the duck takes the farmer a note, Emily inferred, "Now they won't be able to write any more letters to get more things."

Jabberwocky

'Twas brillig, and the slithy toves
Did gyre and gimble in the wabe;
All mimsy were the borogoves,
And the mome raths outgrabe.

"Beware the Jabberwock, my son!
The jaws that bite, the claws that catch!
Beware the Jubjub bird, and shun
The frumious Bandersnatch!"

He took his vorpal sword in hand:
Long time the manxome foe he sought—
So rested he by the Tumtum tree,
And stood awhile in thought.

And, as in uffish thought he stood,
The Jabberwock, with eyes of flame,
Came whiffling through the tulgey wood,
And burbled as it came!

One, two! One, two! And through and through
The vorpal blade went snicker-snack!
He left it dead, and with its head
He went galumphing back.

"And, hast thou slain the Jabberwock?
Come to my arms, my beamish boy!
O frabjous day! Callooh! Callay!"
He chortled in his joy.

'Twas brillig, and the slithy toves
Did gyre and gimble in the wabe;
All mimsy were the borogoves,
And the mome raths outgrabe.

Synthesizing and Summarizing

Given that readers can't store everything they read in their brains, synthesizing and summarizing are important skills to develop. Like the other cognitive strategies we've discussed, synthesizing and summarizing work when the reader returns to the text. Far too often, students miss major points in their syntheses or create summaries that are much too long. The goals of this strategy are accuracy and ownership. The synthesis or summary should be representative of the work and should represent the student's thinking, not the exact words of the author. As such, this strategy is another great example of the importance of the transaction between the text and the reader.

When most students think about synthesizing and summarizing, they think about factual information. Of course, readers do regularly synthesize and summarize expository information. But they should also use this strategy while reading narrative texts. We often hear students start a conversation about fiction with "So, here's what happened so far . . . " For example, Tiffany had read the first two chapters of *The Outsiders* (Hinton, 1967) and reported, "So, here's what happened so far. They have committed a lot of crimes and don't get caught. There is a big conflict between the two groups—greasers and socs. They aren't really gangs, like the ones around here, but they don't get along." She continued synthesizing and summarizing the action from chapters 1 and 2, in her own words and connecting to her experiences.

Monitoring

When understanding is compromised, readers know that they have lost meaning and need to do something about it. Even the most struggling readers know the difference between meaning making and confusion. The difference is that most struggling readers don't know what to do when meaning is lost. Sometimes, the answer is to abandon the book—there really is no point in reading a book that is way too hard. Other times, when the book is a good match, the reader has to reread and determine where meaning was compromised.

There are a number of strategies other than rereading that readers can use to regain meaning, but they all involve some aspect of returning to the text to figure out what went wrong. For example, while reading *Don't Let the Pigeon Drive the Bus!* (Willems, 2003), Nick got confused and didn't understand why the pigeon suddenly was saying, "True story." When he reread a few pages, he realized that he had skipped a page on which the pigeon talks about his cousin driving a bus. While all fix-up strategies are not so easy to implement, Nick's experience highlights the fact that returning to the text is important in regaining meaning. It also highlights the fact that students have to recognize when meaning is lost.

Each of these seven strategies relies on the text, which makes sense because that's what we're trying to do: read! We return to the text, and talk about the text, so that we can gain a better understanding of what we think. Our thoughts develop in an interactive way, based on what the author has said and our own perspectives on the world. As we have noted, there was a time in literary theory when the balance was off and the text drove everything. We wrote this book to address a different issue—namely the misapplication of reader response theory, which allows readers to take off on tangents and not return to the text, so that they ultimately fail to understand what they are reading.

Conclusion

Remembering a good book-club conversation that involved a robust exchange of ideas, we might not think that any participatory rules were in play. However, if we analyze it, we will realize that for this exchange to have occurred, the participants had to have been well aware of how to engage, promote, and support such discourse. Think further about your personal experiences. Whom do you enjoy conversing with? Whom do you enjoy listening to in your book club? It's probably the people who know how to listen and also know how to share well-supported information that both entertains and informs you without dominating the floor.

Building from this analogy, our purpose for writing this book is to use the context of classroom discussion to illustrate the initial and subsequent roles that a text plays as an initiator, extender, evaluator, and illuminator of information. It is critical that students have this understanding if they are to master the content outlined in the Common Core State Standards and be prepared for their college and career experiences. We hope the examples we share will help you expand your understanding of the important role you play as a model and a collaborator. Students will rely on you to support their interactions as they engage with text-based ideas in order to develop and extend their ability to think both widely about many topics and deeply about those they select to focus on. To be able to use these skills long after leaving the context of your classroom, students will need to understand and own the significance of having both an efferent and aesthetic stance as they gather, fully experience, and share in myriad ways textually initiated information in an ever-expanding global world.

CHAPTER 2

Argumentation: Gateway to Text-Based Analysis and Discussion

CONSIDER THE FOLLOWING EXCHANGE, which took place during group-work time in a life sciences class that was studying a botany unit. The students were supposed to be researching the health benefits and claims of food supplements. Bill had heard about Chia seeds, a very popular supplement in California. Amber had not heard of them. They each read a little bit of text from the Internet and started arguing almost immediately:

> **BILL:** But four out of five doctors recommend it.
>
> **AMBER:** So what? That doesn't mean anything.
>
> **BILL:** Yes it does.
>
> **AMBER:** Nah-hah.
>
> **BILL:** Yes-hah.

This squabble is not the type of interaction we're looking for in classrooms where students read like detectives. Bill and Amber had clearly lost their ability to share their perspectives, provide evidence and claims, offer counterclaims, and disagree without being disagreeable. They did not return to the text to analyze the author's perspectives, nor did they attempt to synthesize this new information with any they had gleaned from publications they had read previously. If they had, their conversation would have been different. They might have sounded more like their peers, who had experience with argumentation:

> **BRAD:** I know that this sounds kinda gross, but fish oil seems like it does help people. My grandma swears it works.
>
> **CHELSEA:** Really, they get oil from fish and people eat that?

BRAD: It's more like a pill you take. It says here that people need omega-3 fatty acids and that fish are a good source of these.

CHELSEA: Where did you find that?

BRAD: There are lots of websites, but this one I'm reading is from Wikipedia. Go to this page and read it (tells her the webpage).

CHELSEA: Wait, look at the top of the page. It says that this page has inappropriate or misinterpreted citations. I'm not sure that this is a good source. Let's find a different one.

BRAD: Good point.

CHELSEA: I'm not saying that you're wrong about fish oil, but I think we should find a better source. And why are you thinking about fish oil anyway? We're supposed to be talking about plants— it's botany, remember?

BRAD: But that's the great thing. Fish don't make omega-3 fatty acids. They store them from the microalgae they eat. And there it is—the plant connection!

In this exchange, the students had a productive conversation that led them to greater understanding of the content. They referred back to the text and made connections between their own experiences and what they were reading. They also realized that they needed additional sources and proceeded to search for them. In other words, these middle school students used argumentation in their conversation, and this allowed them to go deeper into the content and gain greater understanding.

Exploring Argumentation

When we hear the word *argument*, we probably think of children bickering in the sandbox over a toy, or perhaps a couple engaged in a heated discussion about a personal matter. That's the common use of the term, but a more formal definition is used in academic circles. An *argument* is a way of assembling information logically so that the reader or listener can draw conclusions. We draw conclusions each day as we weigh the positions of political candidates, make decisions about our health, and prioritize work and recreational activities. Students are also required to draw conclusions as they read texts, write coherent papers, and contribute to classroom discussions.

Much of what students understand in the texts they read and write comes from their participation in discussion. *Collaborative argumentation* is a field of study that focuses on how learners co-construct meaning in the company of peers. The social aspect of collaborative argumentation is vital for learning, as participants make claims, provide evidence, and consider the counterclaims of others (Nussbaum, 2008). In order for readers to understand argumentation well when reading, they first must know how to use argumentation during discussions and also in their writing.

Keefer, Zeitz, and Resnick (2000) studied the dialogue of fourth-grade students as they engaged in small-group discussions of stories that their teacher had read aloud to them. The researchers were interested in identifying the ways in which the discussions evolved and determining whether students gained a deeper understanding of the text through discussion. These students had been taught about the importance of using the text to support their claims. Keefer and his colleagues found that as the year progressed, student discussions about texts became richer and more productive, and comprehension of the text increased after the discussion. They note that "productive literary discussions require participants to consider textual events and literary meanings and, eventually, to discuss differing interpretations of these events and meanings. This suggests that productive literary discussions are likely to include a relatively high proportion of interpretive literary content in the argumentation" (Keefer, Zeitz, & Resnick, 2000, p. 78).

In this chapter, we will explore the topic of argumentation and its application in rhetoric and logic. Although these terms are often associated with older students, we will explain how argumentation can and should be fostered with younger students as they analyze texts and engage in discussions with their teachers and peers. Evidence of students' abilities to use argumentation can be found in their writing. We will conclude the chapter with an examination of accountable talk and language frames to support these discussions.

X-Raying the Book to Find Its Argumentation Bones

In their classic *How to Read a Book*, first published in 1940, Adler and Van Doren (1940/1972) tell us, "Every book has a skeleton hidden between its covers. Your job as an analytic reader is to find it" (p. 75). The authors advise readers to "x-ray the book" to locate its arguments. They go on to say that while some writers make it easier for you by summarizing arguments in one neat paragraph, most do not. They further explain that x-raying means looking at the text at three levels: terms, propositions, and arguments. Terms—what we think of as "word choice"—can reveal the author's intent. For instance, the choice of the word *fight* rather than *disagreement* sets the stage for what is likely to come next. Propositions can be thought of as assumptions that may or may not be absolute: "The sky is dark at night" is indisputable, but "The night sky is threatened by light pollution" is debatable. Finally, the argument is a series of statements supported by evidence.

We can see all three levels functioning in the following sample passage:

> *Astronomers and security experts disagree on the need for regulations that affect the level of light pollution in the night sky. Astronomers say that it has become more difficult in recent decades to study the stars, while security specialists assert that crime is reduced in well-lit areas. But increased attention to energy consumption is giving both sides pause. A recent report stated that 25% of the world's energy consumption is dedicated to lighting.*

When we wrote this passage, we selected the terms *disagree* and *light pollution* to juxtapose the civility of the debate against a more emotionally charged condition. The propositions include the necessity of darkness in astronomy and the equally pressing need for light in crime prevention. Then the author previews the argument by introducing information about energy consumption. A discussion of this paragraph alone can prepare readers for the more technical information that will follow.

Of course, students don't read for information only. Narrative texts fill our classrooms and our lives. Argumentation is at the heart of Atticus Finch's speech to the jury in *To Kill a Mockingbird* (Lee, 1960) and of the boy wizard's final confrontation with the evil Voldemort in *Harry Potter and the Deathly Hallows* (Rowling, 2007). Even among younger readers who are not yet writing formal essays, the ability to recognize argumentation is essential for x-raying the text to expose its conceptual structure. Understanding how other authors present a balanced, well-thought-out, and well-supported argument provides a model from which students can draw when they do attempt to present an argument in written form. Even before crafting a written argument understanding the language, examples, and persuasive techniques writers employ to support a character's argument as more than a black or white opinion, helps one understand how to convey his own spoken argument. Examining argumentation in text allows the reader to develop an understanding that there is no "right side" to the focused issue but rather that a sophisticated thinker, speaker, and writer entertains multiple points of view while contextualizing information to support the presentation of a reasoned, supported, and balanced position.

This understanding of people's writing through the authors they read was illustrated in Jane Hansen's (2001) book, *When Writers Read*, when the author says, "my understanding of reading came when I studied writers" (p. 2). She observes that "when writers read, they evaluate differently than nonwriters do. . . . When writers read their own work, they realize how much their readers don't know. Later, when they read something written by another writer, they know how much is missing and wonder about the decisions that writer made" (p. 2).

Argumentation is an essential part of persuasion, but also more than just persuasion. *Persuasive writing* is about convincing the reader to agree with the writer's point of view. We see it in advertisements, political cartoons, and even propaganda.

But persuasive writing doesn't necessarily require that the information be accurate or complete. Persuasive techniques include the use of glittering generalities and card stacking, such as when a company says you'll "feel cleaner" if you use its product. Argumentation, on the other hand, requires a formal application of logic that depends on reason and evidence (Hillocks, 2010). The rhetoric of argumentation is based on leading the reader through a series of logical steps that end with a conclusion that has been built on a foundation of information.

The use of the word *rhetoric* is purposeful. It is derived from the Greek word for *oration* and was originally applied to the spoken word. The term has since evolved to include written language as well and describes the effective communication of ideas and concepts. Our focus on rhetoric in the context of text-based discussions encompasses oral as well as written language. Teaching students to read texts rhetorically and discuss them using rhetorical devices is essential for fostering academically challenging discourse.

Reading Rhetorically

Reading like a detective requires that students read not only to extract information but also to interrogate, or x-ray, the text to determine the ways the author has presented that information. To read rhetorically, one needs a healthy dose of skepticism and a belief that the reader's role is an active one. Students read rhetorically when they question the text, determine the author's purpose, consider sources, and challenge the message. Not every text demands this level of inspection, but exposure to and experience with narrative and informational texts that invite rhetorical reading are necessary to build critical thinking.

The Common Core State Standards emphasize that reading and writing rhetorically are necessary skills for college and career readiness. Students should be able to "write logical arguments based on substantive claims, sound reasoning, and relevant evidence" (National Governors Association, 2010, p. 2). Of course, students don't magically write this way. They must first be exposed to the ways other writers use argumentation so that they can incorporate these techniques into their own writing. When young writers pick up rhetorical skills from mentor texts, it is analogous to "watching someone dance and then secretly, in your own room, trying out a few steps" (Prose, 2006, p. 9).

Bean, Chappell, and Gillam (2011) explain that reading rhetorically entails an inquiry into three factors: purpose, audience, and genre. The reader asks three simple but powerful questions:

1. What purpose?

2. What audience?

3. In what genre?

A webpage about the brain that was produced by a company marketing a memory-boosting game should be approached differently from a passage about the brain in a high school biology textbook or a poem that contemplates the brain. Each has a different audience (presumably the game is for middle-aged adults battling the first signs of aging, whereas the biology textbook is aimed at a younger crowd). Another example is Emily Dickinson's untitled poem (Life CXXVI) that opens with the line, "The brain is wider than the sky." This poem appeals to another audience altogether and would not be read to glean the latest advances in the neurosciences. In each case, the author's purpose, the intended audience, and the genre (advertisement, textbook, and poem) influence the way in which the words should be understood. It is important to note that even in the case of the advertisement, the information may be accurate. The intent of reading rhetorically is not to criticize and condemn but rather to take each of these factors into proper account.

Second-grade teacher Claudia Shinn uses an approach similar to that shared in the previous paragraph when she teaches about precipitation and evaporation in her science class. Students compare and contrast two texts to determine purpose, audience, and genre. The first is a Navajo folktale about a frog that quenches a volcano with water, called *Frog Brings Rain* (Powell, 2006). The second is an informational book called *Where Does the Water Go?* (Lucca, 2001). While each book offers an explanation of cloud formation and rain, only the latter one provides scientific information. Ms. Shinn invites discussion about both books by asking questions about purpose, audience, and genre:

MS. SHINN: I'm noticing that both of these books are really different from each other. Let's talk about why the authors wrote these. We can start with *Frog Brings Rain*.

AVERIL: It's more like a story.

RICARDO: Like what you read before bed.

MS. SHINN: Is that why the author wrote this?

JOSEPH: Nah, not that. I think he wrote it for 'splaining.

AVERIL: For how the rain got started.

MS. SHINN: What are your clues?

LYNDA: There's a First Man and a First Woman, so it's a long time ago. At the beginning of the world.

RICARDO: And there's no fire department.

AVERIL: And the animals can talk.

MS. SHINN: Right, and they can't talk in real life. Take a look at the end of the book, too. I see an important clue. (The students flip to the last pages and reread.)

LYNDA: She [the author] says why the clouds make rain.

JOSEPH: It's a lesson.

MS. SHINN: That's really important in a folktale, isn't it? A folktale usually has an important lesson, or an explanation, like you said before. So did the author write this to tell you about rain?

AVERIL: No, it's for a good story. She knew we'd like it!

The class turns its attention to the informational book and holds a similar discussion about the purpose and genre. They also discuss the audience and agree that both books are written for children their age, but for different reasons. In the second book, there are terms such as *evaporation* and *water cycle*. The students note the differences in the art, contrasting the illustrations in the first book with the photographs in the second. The class agrees that the authors' purposes differ as well: the first book is intended to entertain, and the second, to provide scientific information.

These discussions form the first steps in exploring argumentation in texts. In the next section, we'll consider how authors use formal logic in texts to create arguments that persuade, enlighten, and at times, inspire.

Using Ethos, Pathos, and Logos in Argumentation

The study of logic reaches back to the time of the Greek philosophers, especially Aristotle and Socrates. Many of us were exposed to logic in math class when we were taught how geometric proofs are constructed. Computer programs are written using a series of logical steps that lead to the performance of a function. Science lab experiments also follow a formal line of logic that leads to an expected outcome. When the experiment does not yield anticipated results, the scientist reviews each step and questions the logic on which it was predicated, looking for the flaw that led to the experiment's failure.

Whereas logic in mathematics and science involves absolute truths, logic in most disciplines in the humanities does not. Rhetorical arguments use three modes of persuasion: *ethos, pathos,* and *logos.* These modes extend back to Aristotle and are evidenced in persuasive writing, such as opinion pieces, as well as in argumentation.

The first mode, ethos, appeals to the reader based on the authority or honesty of the writer. This chapter has employed ethos each time it has used direct quotes from noted authorities on the topic of rhetoric and argumentation. The usefulness of ethos is dependent on the reader's knowledge of the writer's expertise. In some cases, the writer adds identifiers such as "well-known astronomer" or "Nobel Laureate poet" to enhance the reader's understanding of the weight of the information.

The second mode of persuasion is pathos. Just as we commonly use the word today, *pathos* refers to an appeal to the emotions. When Atticus Finch makes his courtroom speech, he uses pathos as a means for persuading the jury:

> But there is one way in this country in which all men are created equal— there is one human institution that makes a pauper the equal of a Rockefeller, the stupid man the equal of an Einstein, and the ignorant man the equal of any college president. That institution, gentlemen, is a court. It can be the Supreme Court of the United States or the humblest J.P. court in the land, or this honorable court, which you serve. (Lee, 1960, p. 339)

This portion of Finch's closing argument evokes concepts of democracy, justice, and American ideals about the everyman to appeal to the jury's emotional logic. It is important to note that the logic of pathos is not devoid of content. Appeals to the reader's sense of right and wrong invite them to consider the morals and ethics of a situation. Texts intended to inspire social justice use pathos to support a call to action.

For example, Mr. Cleveland's sixth-grade students discussed the use of pathos during a reading of *Left for Dead* (Nelson, 2003), the story of eleven-year-old Hunter Scott's quest to exonerate the captain of the *USS Indianapolis*. The ship was sunk while on a secret mission during World War II, and many of the sailors perished from shark attacks during the four days they were in the water. Captain McVay was court-martialed. Scott became interested in the case while doing a social studies research project, and he testified before Congress in 1999, sharing new evidence of the captain's innocence. The Congressional committee later officially exonerated McVay. Here's an excerpt from the class discussion:

RANDY:	Wow, that was amazing. I can't believe a kid could be the one to do all that.
MR. CLEVELAND:	Let's take a look at the section of the book about his testimony to Congress. It starts on page 170. (Students turn to this page.)
BRIAN:	I remember reading this. He was really strong about his convictions.
MR. CLEVELAND:	How did he do that?
BRIAN:	He told them (reading), "I have learned that democracy is a treasure so valued, men and women are willing to give up their lives in its pursuit."
OSCAR:	(joining in on the reading) "I know eight hundred eighty men of the *USS Indianapolis* made the supreme sacrifice. I pray that some of those who gave their lives are looking down on what I'm doing at this moment with a smile, knowing their sacrifice was not in vain."
MR. CLEVELAND:	Talk about that. What's Hunter doing in that moment? Why is it so effective?

DOMINIQUE: He's using an emotional argument. Like talking about democracy and telling the congressman that he's praying to the dead sailors.

RANDY: And in the next paragraph, he shows them the dog tags of the dead captain. It's hard to get past that.

DOMINIQUE: But he's got evidence, too. Look on 169. He talks about how he contacted all the survivors and did a survey with them, and it was unanimous that they thought the captain shouldn't have been court-martialed.

Dominique has identified the third type of appeal, called *logos*. These arguments are based on logic and are primarily fact driven. Academic writing is mostly logos in nature. The use of quantitative information is a chief example of logos. Hunter Scott strengthened his logos argument by including an ethos element—he surveyed survivors of the tragedy, making it far more meaningful than if the surveys had been done with sailors who were not on the *USS Indianapolis* that day in 1944.

MR. CLEVELAND: Keep going. You're on to something.

DOMINIQUE: He's got some good facts. Like on page 171. He talks about the coded documents . . .

OSCAR: . . . that showed he asked for an escort ship . . .

RANDY: . . . and sent distress signals as soon as they got torpedoed . . .

DOMINIQUE: . . . but no one answered.

MR. CLEVELAND: Sounds like you're convinced. Did Congress make the right decision?

For the next ten minutes, Mr. Cleveland and the small group of students discussed the details of the case, citing the evidence Hunter Scott and the survivors submitted to Congress. They also discussed the fact that as a collaborator, sharing his perspective, the book would cast a favorable light on the experiences. Over the next day, the boys did further research online, visiting the Wikipedia entries for "Scott" and the "*USS Indianapolis*," as well as the website of a nonprofit organization dedicated to the ship. This website also had a link to the official Congressional testimony, so the students were able to view the proceedings in their entirety. This example illustrates how these students' examination of the modes of argumentation used in the book spurred their desire to find additional information about the case.

Similar investigations and resulting conversations often occur at the high school level. For example, each fall, Ms. Enriquez introduces her ninth-grade health sciences students to the legal, ethical, and moral considerations of controversial health-related topics. Like Mr. Cleveland, Ms. Enriquez wants her students to understand that personal opinions are not enough; they need to also consider a broader range of information. As part of this process, students select a topic of their choosing to read about and discuss with peers. Examples include cosmetic surgery for teenagers, genetic selection to create "designer" babies, and euthanasia. Students use a graphic organizer like the one in figure 2.1 to prepare for small-group discussions of their topic and then later to prepare for an analytic research paper they will write. Each year as the course unfolds, we are amazed at how the students' initial opinion-based responses expand to include expert accounts, data-supported arguments, and contrastive positions as a result of engaging with multiple text sources and conversations with their peers and teachers.

Name: _____

Planning Grid for Your Research Paper: "The Legal and Ethical Issues of _____ _____ "

SOURCE	What are the LAWS governing this issue?	What are the pro-fessional ETHICS for this issue?	What are the MORAL arguments in favor of this issue?	What are the MORAL arguments against this issue?

Figure 2.1: Planning tool for student paper.

Teaching Toulmin's Model of Argument

Students can learn to write formal arguments through the use of an argumentation model developed by Stephen Toulmin (1958). This model provides students with ideas about how to formulate an argument, not a formula for an argument. This is an important distinction. Students should be taught the following six elements of argument so that they can both analyze the perspective of someone else's argument and create their own.

1. **The claim.** This is the initial stance taken by the writer and contains the conclusion he or she wants you to draw. Example: *You should read every day.*

2. **The grounds.** These are the facts, statistics, and information that support the claim and typically employ ethos, pathos, or logos. Example: *Students who read for at least fifteen minutes a day are more likely to score in the eightieth percentile on standardized tests.*

3. **The warrant.** This is the bridge between the claim and the grounds, as the writer explains why the information is relevant to the argument. Example: *Daily reading in and out of school is an easy way to improve achievement.*

4. **The backing.** This is additional information that, while not as strong as the grounds, supports the claim. Example: *Most of the classrooms in this school have a sustained silent reading program that makes it possible for students to start a daily reading plan.*

5. **The qualifier.** The word *most* in the previous example is a qualifier. Other qualifiers include *sometimes*, *almost*, and *at least*. An argument that fails to accurately acknowledge limitations can be readily dismissed.

6. **The rebuttal.** This statement may come after a counterargument or in anticipation of one. Example: *Finding a book should never be a problem. The school library has many books available for all kinds of readers who are interested in all kinds of topics. The librarian is always available to help students find a good book that's just right for him or her.*

Admittedly, some students can get lost in the elements of Toulmin's argumentation model, especially if they are younger or are struggling readers and writers. When teachers use Toulmin's model as a writing *formula*, students get bogged down trying to comply with the six elements and do not learn the art and science of argumentation. Rex, Thomas, and Engel (2010) work with students at an alternative high school, some of whom have difficulty putting their good ideas onto paper. They teach students about argumentation using just three elements: stance, evidence, and warrant. Students adopt a stance on a topic, provide evidence to support that stance, and explain why the evidence is linked to the claim. The authors provide thinking points for students as they consider adopting a stance (fig. 2.2, page 38) and finding supporting evidence (fig. 2.3, page 38).

WHAT DO WE MEAN BY STANCE?

Three questions can help one deliberately choose a stance to take for a particular situation with specific readers:

1. **Point of view:** How do I see and understand what I'm looking at?

   What in my experience makes me care about this issue, idea, circumstance, or condition?

   How does this way of caring influence me toward thinking about it?

   How does my relationship with my readers and my current situation influence where I stand?

2. **Claim:** What is true and should be known about this subject?

   What is important to understand about this issue, idea, circumstance, or condition for this situation at this moment?

3. **Request:** What should readers understand about this subject?

   What would or should readers think is important?

   How would or should they feel?

   How would or should they act?

Source: Rex, Thomas, & Engel (2010), p. 57. Used with permission.

Figure 2.2: Helping students think about stance.

WHAT SHOULD WE KNOW ABOUT EVIDENCE?

Evidence that is believable and convincing should satisfy four conditions:

1. **Is the evidence credible?**

   Does the evidence match your readers' experience of the world? If not, does the evidence come from a source that readers would accept as more knowledgeable or authoritative than they are?

2. **Is the evidence sufficient?**

   Does the argument provide enough evidence to convince the readers? Consider the profiles of different readers and how much evidence they would require to understand the applicability of the evidence.

Figure 2.3: Helping students think about evidence.

3. **Is the evidence accurate?**

Is the evidence valid or trustworthy? Are the sources quoted authoritative in their field? Are statistics gathered in verifiable ways from good sources? Are quotations complete and fair (not out of context)? Are facts verifiable from other sources?

4. **Which order of evidence is best?**

Evidence should be arranged in the order that seems most reasonable so as to be most forceful. Each piece of evidence should gain strength as it builds upon previous evidence, creating a forceful argument. Why is one ordering of evidence the best of all the options?

Source: Rex, Thomas, & Engel (2010), p. 58. Used with permission.

In our high school health sciences course, the students choose a controversial health topic and spend time in small-group discussions analyzing the arguments forwarded by writers of essays, websites, and textbooks. Then we give them an assignment to write an analytic research paper on the topic that requires them to present both sides of the argument without forwarding a stance of their own (see fig. 2.4, page 40). For example, Raymond chose the topic of reporting genetic health risks to employers. He included legal claims ("An employer can screen for genetic problems, but that is illegal if it is done without the person's consent"). He also noted that there were ethical issues both for and against such testing:

> According to the Department of Labor, there were cases in the 1970s of African-Americans being screened for sickle cell anemia and then not being hired because it could cost the company more money if they had a child with the disease. But the Markkula Center for Applied Ethics says that genetic screening might prevent people who are more susceptible from getting cancer from the workplace.

The purpose for this assignment is to encourage students to look outward for reasoned information on both sides of an issue and not simply draw on their own opinions of a topic. We require students to cite at least six reputable sources of information as they explore the chosen issue. By analyzing texts for argument and discussing them with peers, students begin to appreciate the complexities and nuances of the issues they face in health care.

WHAT IS AN ANALYTIC RESEARCH PAPER?

An analytic research paper highlights a particular issue or problem. The paper focuses on analysis of the issue and its solutions. The posture of the writer is that of a neutral observer more than an advocate for a particular position. The success of the paper is based on how completely and clearly the writer has identified the key aspects of the issue and the significance to the field to which they relate.

Your analytic paper is about a controversial issue in the health care field, and you will choose the topic you would like to research. We encourage you to talk with your family about what you are learning and find out what they think about the topic. This will help you to understand the complexities of the moral arguments for and against the issue you have selected. Suggested topics include:

- Stem cell research
- Assisted suicide
- Euthanasia
- Choosing your baby's gender and/or other traits ("designer babies")
- Genetic engineering
- Gene therapy
- Cloning
- Abortion
- Assisted fertilization
- Gender reassignment surgery
- Adoption by gay couples
- Cosmetic surgery for minors
- Reporting genetic health risks to employers and insurance companies
- Others?

Here are the quick facts about your analytic research paper:

1. The paper includes complete and factual information about each of these three elements: Legal Aspects, Professional Ethics, and Moral Arguments For and Against.
2. Each of these elements is supported by at least two credible sources of information (book, encyclopedia, website).

Figure 2.4: Assignment for analytic research paper.

3. A Works Cited page contains each of these sources, using MLA style.
4. The paper is typed, double-spaced, Times or Times New Roman font (12 pt.); it is 2–4 pages in length, not counting the Works Cited page.
5. The paper contains title, author's name (yours), and headings to organize it.
6. The work is original, and your own.

Source: Frey, Fisher, & Gonzalez (2010), pp. 56–57.

Teaching Accountable Talk

A challenge for any teacher is to get students to listen and respond to their peers through meaningful conversations. Despite teachers' efforts, students tend to identify the teacher as the primary discussant, diminishing the attention they could otherwise devote to other participants. The result is less a discussion than a series of individual exchanges in which the teacher is always the common denominator. One reason for this tendency is that it is the teacher who directs the discussion, but another factor is that students have far less experience talking with one another using academic discourse than they do with the teacher.

The idea behind accountable talk (Resnick, 2000) is that students use a framework for listening and responding, pressing for evidence, asking for clarification, building on one another's ideas, and providing information. These principles constitute a set of norms about the way verbal interactions will occur and provide guidelines to help students maintain a high level of academic discourse. We call it "disagreeing without being disagreeable." Accountable talk practices apply to paired, small-group, and whole-class discussions. Students have three commitments to community, knowledge, and reasoning:

1. Stay on topic.
2. Use information that is accurate and appropriate for the topic.
3. Think deeply about what the partner has to say. (Fisher & Frey, 2007, p. 23)

In addition to adhering to the basic norms of conversation, students in classrooms using accountable talk are required to use reasoning and information to formulate arguments (Michaels, O'Connor, & Resnick, 2008). They are taught to provide coherent explanations, justify their answers, provide evidence, answer questions raised by others, and incorporate the responses of others in their discussions. Conversely, when listening to others, they are encouraged to ask questions, request clarification, challenge misconceptions, and suggest counterclaims. The purpose is for students to jointly create knowledge using extended discourse and dialogue.

The teacher is not a bystander in these conversations. Indeed, he or she models the kinds of conversational moves that are the hallmark of accountable talk. When students are first learning to use accountable talk, the teacher can reflect back to students what they are doing in order to draw their attention to these moves. Consider the ways first-grade teacher Constance Harrington used this technique as she and her students discussed *Miss Nelson Is Missing!* (Allard, 1977):

JAZMINE: When Miss Nelson was absent and the kids were acting bad, they seemed like they were having fun at first.

DEON: Like when we was bad for the sub.

MS. HARRINGTON: How could you tell the children were having fun?

DEON: (pointing to picture) Their faces is all happy and all.

JAZMINE: Yeah, like look at this kid here (points to a portion of the illustration).

MS. HARRINGTON: I can see you're both using each other's ideas. That's what people do when they're having important conversations. Let's get some other ideas in here. Ali, did the children always feel like they were having fun, or did that change?

ALL: No! They wanted their old teacher back.

MS. HARRINGTON: Show us in the book where that happened. (Turning to the other students) I'm asking him that question because that helps all of us understand his idea that the children's opinion changed.

Ms. Harrington is taking on an active role in the discussion by stating aloud the conversational turns that are occurring in the group. Over time, she facilitates more conversation among students so that she can reduce the number of comments that are directed at her alone. Much of this facilitation initially occurs in partner conversations, using language frames to further scaffold discussion.

Framing the Argument

Students gaining argumentation skills in discussion and writing benefit from scaffolds. One of our favorite ways to support students is through the use of *language frames*. These are a series of partial sentences that serve as the academic language for explaining, clarifying, and providing evidence. The intent is for students to incorporate such conversational moves in their oral and written discourse. Composition instructors Graff and Birkenstein (2006) call them templates and describe them as a path for sequencing ideas so that they can persuade and illuminate. For example, after his students read two opposing opinion pieces on school discipline, seventh-grade teacher Matt Hendricks provided the following language frame to guide students' text-based discussions (Frey & Fisher, 2011):

> *According to this article, a zero tolerance policy is (necessary/ unnecessary) because _____. First, the author states that _____. In addition, the author argues that _____. I agree with the author's claim that _____. However, I disagree with the claim that _____. In my opinion, _____. What's your opinion?*

Extended language frames like this one are useful because they assist students with developing a rational sequence of thinking. Students tend to struggle with laying out a reasonable argument that follows a logical path from one point to the next. Mr. Hendricks's language frame gave students a means for examining claims and counter-claims in the two articles. After their initial discussion, he provided a second language frame to scaffold the students' understanding of how claims and evidence are linked. This frame also encouraged students to go back to the article to cite a direct quote:

> *The author of the article titled _____ said that zero tolerance policies are necessary/unnecessary because _____. The author said that one reason was because _____. A second reason is because _____. The author said that these are good reasons to support continuing/banning zero tolerance policies because _____."*

These language frames will later scaffold written language, as students organize their summaries of the articles (first frame) by citing reasons and evidence (second frame). In their writing, the students will also use a third frame to employ ethos by establishing the article author's expertise on the subject:

> *The author of this article is known for his/her work as _____ and has _____ years of experience in the field of _____.*

Argumentation language frames are also useful in other content areas, such as science. Because of the importance of inquiry in science learning, students need to learn how to question results, processes, and one another. Fourth-grade science teacher Karen Jessop uses language frames as part of her think-aloud process (Davey, 1983). As Ms. Jessop observes, follows a lab sheet, or reads a passage from the textbook, she models her use of argumentation, which we have emphasized:

> *When I first read this paragraph about the way the compass works,* I thought about my experience *with using one on a hike I took on Mount Shasta.* I noticed that *no matter which way I turned, the needle always pointed north. But I didn't always want to go north, so at first* I thought this was confusing. *But the guide on my hiking trip showed me that I could turn the compass housing so it pointed in the direction I wanted to go.* In this paragraph, it says *that the compass needle always points north because of the magnetic north pole.* I wonder what would happen if *I had something made of iron in my pocket while I was on the hike?*

Ms. Jessop uses many other language frames, which appear in figure 2.5. We organized these frames to highlight the elements of argumentation that they address.

Making a claim	I observed _____ when _____.
	I compared _____ and _____.
	I noticed _____, when _____.
	The effect of _____ on _____ is _____.
Providing evidence	The evidence I use to support _____ is _____.
	I believe _____ (statement) because _____ (justification).
	I know that _____ is _____ because _____.
	Based on _____, I think _____.
	Based on _____, my hypothesis is _____.
Asking for evidence	I have a question about _____.
	Does _____ have additional information about _____?
	What causes _____ to _____?
	Can you show me where you found the information about _____?
Offering a counterclaim	I disagree with _____ because _____.
	The reason I believe _____ is _____.
	The facts that support my idea are _____.
	In my opinion, _____.
	One difference between my idea and yours is _____.

Figure 2.5: Language frames for argumentation in science.

Inviting speculation	I wonder what would happen if _____.
	I have a question about _____.
	Let's find out how we can test these samples for _____.
	We want to test _____ to find out if _____.
	If I change _____ (variable in experiment), then I think _____ will happen, because _____.
	I wonder why _____.
	What caused _____?
	How would this be different if _____?
	What do you think will happen if _____?
	What do you think will happen next?
Reaching consensus	I agree that _____ because _____.
	How would this be different if _____?
	We all have the same idea about _____.

Source: Ross, Fisher, & Frey (2009), p. 29. Used with permission.

Conclusion

Without a deep understanding of argumentation, students fail to x-ray the text and determine the ways in which the author constructed it. Reading like a detective applies to all types of text, from traditional print to song lyrics, websites, graphic novels, and the range of readings students encounter throughout their day. Again, we are not suggesting that students read only to analyze what the author says but rather that they base their discussions and writing on the interplay between what the author wrote and their own experiences. Having said that, without understanding the audience, genre, and purpose, students are unlikely to be able to read deeply enough to make meaning. Instead, they scratch the surface of the text, often missing the opportunity to engage deeply with their own ideas. And the ability to disrupt this confusion is what the authors of the Common Core State Standards suggest is missing from the instruction shared in many classrooms. One of their "College and Career Readiness Anchor Standards" states that students should be able to "read closely to determine what the text says explicitly and to make logical inferences from it; cite specific textual evidence when writing or speaking to support conclusions drawn from the text" (Common Core State Standards Initiative, 2010).

There are a number of ways to help students develop their argumentation skills so that they can read closely. Of course, each of these concepts must be taught. As teachers, we can use logic, Toulmin's model, accountable talk, and language frames to apprentice students into this type of thinking and discussion. When entire schools reach consensus on the teaching of argumentation, students progress faster and develop habits that transfer from grade to grade and classroom to classroom.

Lincoln School District in Rhode Island has developed a schoolwide rubric for the implementation of text-based discussions (see fig. 2.6, page 47). This self-assessment tool identifies key indicators of success in four areas: conduct, speaking and reasoning, listening, and reading. When students receive regular exposure to the skills described in the rubric, they begin to critically examine texts and clarify their understandings of the information they read. As a result, in their arguments—whether vocal or written—they develop the ability to identify competing positional alternatives, acknowledge that most positions are highly complex, and conclude by presenting well-researched data and established criteria that support the plausibility of their topical stance.

In using the materials and instruction we have described in this chapter, our end goal is to lead our students to realize that their stance on a topic, at any given time, is merely one well-documented position. We also hope that through our intentional instruction and our modeling of the power of inquiry of text, self, and colleagues, they will develop as critical thinkers who are open to the possibility that their stance may become better supported or altered as additional topical information and insight become available. As the 21st century unfolds before them, we anticipate that students will use their abilities as critical thinkers to seek expanded understandings from the many voices shared through the myriad new-media texts available to them. Only then will their arguments truly make far-reaching differences for the world.

Text-Based Discussion Schoolwide Rubric

Name: _____   Score: _____   Teacher Name: _____

Expectations	Exceeds Standard 4	Meets Standard 3	Nearly Meets Standard 2	Below Standard 1
Conduct	Demonstrates respect for the learning process by showing patience with different and complex ideas. Shows initiative by asking for clarification and bringing others into the conversation. Speaks to all participants to deepen understanding of the topic.	Shows respect and patience for a range of individual ideas by participating in group discussions. Makes insightful comments and brings others into the conversation by utilizing logical organization and language, appropriate to audience, context, and purpose. Addresses most comments to other participants to encourage further discussion.	Shows little respect and patience for individual ideas when participating in group discussions. Makes relevant comments and attempts to bring others into the conversation but is too forceful or too shy and does not contribute to the progress of the conversation. Most comments are directed toward the teacher; most comments do not encourage further dialogue.	Shows no respect and patience for ideas when participating in group discussions. Uses inappropriate language. Does not contribute to and/or limits dialogue (for example, argumentative).
Speaking and Reasoning	Supports thesis with many well-chosen details and provides an insightful conclusion by making many connections between ideas and resolves contradictory concepts. Insightful analysis considers multiple alternative viewpoints (anticipates and addresses potential problems, mistakes, or misunderstandings that might arise for the audience).	Supports thesis with well-chosen details and provides a coherent conclusion by making some connections between ideas and/or resolving contradictory concepts. Analysis is logical and considers some alternative viewpoints (anticipates and addresses potential problems, mistakes, or misunderstandings that might arise for the audience).	Attempts to support thesis with some details and provide a coherent conclusion but makes few connections between ideas and fails to resolve contradictory concepts. Uses limited logical analysis and/or fails to consider alternative viewpoints.	Does not support thesis and makes no connection between ideas and fails to resolve contradictory concepts. No analysis is evident and fails to consider alternative viewpoints.

(continued) ↓

Figure 2.6: Schoolwide rubric for text-based discussion.

Expectations	Exceeds standard 4	Meets standard 3	Nearly meets standard 2	Below standard 1
Listening	Consistently demonstrates active listening by effectively summarizing, paraphrasing, questioning, or contributing to information presented. Points out faulty logic and ignores all distractions. Reaches a consensus with the group to solve a problem, make a decision, or achieve a goal.	Consistently demonstrates active listening by accurately summarizing, paraphrasing, questioning, or contributing to information presented. Maintains consistent focus by identifying and evaluating the essential elements of the discussion and pointing out some faulty logic and ignoring most distractions. Reaches a consensus with the group to solve a problem, make a decision, or achieve a goal.	Demonstrates some active listening, but may contain inaccuracies or contribute to misunderstandings. Attempts to maintain a consistent focus by identifying and evaluating the essential elements of the discussion, but fails to point out some faulty logic and appears distracted. Attempts to reach a consensus, but is unable to agree with all aspects of the solution of the group.	Limited responses demonstrate little listening. Unaware of faulty logic and is inattentive and distracted. Does not reach consensus with the group.
Reading	Demonstrates thorough familiarity with the text by drawing insightful inferences, including ones about author's purpose. Demonstrates exceptional comprehension strategies by making multiple, accurate references to specific parts of the text to answer questions, to state the main/central ideas, and/or to provide supporting details.	Demonstrates familiarity with the text by drawing inferences, including one about author's purpose. Demonstrates comprehension strategies by making accurate references to the text to answer questions, to state the main/central ideas, and/or to provide supporting details.	Demonstrates limited familiarity with the text with limited inferences concerning author's purpose. Demonstrates limited comprehension strategies by making few references to the text.	Demonstrates no familiarity with the text. Demonstrates no comprehension strategy with no references to the text.

Source: Lincoln School District, Lincoln, RI. Used with permission.

CHAPTER 3

Analyzing and Discussing Narrative Texts

"I CAN JUST PICTURE THIS. There's our main man, Romeo, standing on the street. He's talking with Juliet, but she doesn't know who's talking. I know this because he says, 'My name, dear saint, is hateful to myself / Because it is an enemy to thee,' and I'm thinking that he doesn't want to be recognized because of the family problems. He wants to talk with her, but he knows that he can't. How would you feel if you wanted to tell someone that you liked them but were afraid to?" asks ninth-grade English teacher Cindy Lin. The students immediately turn to one another and make a text-to-self connection, which redirects the focal point from Romeo and Juliet to the students' life experiences:

> **JUAN:** I had that happen to me. I didn't want to talk to the parents because they didn't like me, maybe because I'm Mexican.
>
> **ALLISON:** Really? I thought it was just me. For me, it was because of my hair. Remember when I dyed it bright red?

As evidenced by their comments, these two students comprehended the text and were, therefore, able to make personal connections with a piece of literature written centuries before they were born. But their teacher knows that although text-to-self connections are important as an invitation into a text, the students' conversation shouldn't end without returning to the text and figuring out what the author is saying. She knows that if she does not redirect the discussion to the text, the students could easily continue focusing on personal experiences, and Shakespeare's words would be lost. To model for them that it is important to return to the text after making a personal connection, Ms. Lin asks, "Why does the author include this dialogue? What's the purpose for having this as part of the scene?" The students' responses show that Ms. Lin's question has shifted their attention back to the text:

> **JUAN:** I think it's a reminder that the families have trouble with each other. Remember, before, when we learned about them hating each other?

ALLISON: But even right here, Juliet says, "Deny thy father and refuse thy name." She doesn't know he's listening, but we keep getting reminders about the family problems. I think that is going to be really important later.

In our English classes, the teachers read books aloud and model their thinking so that students see the give-and-take, back-and-forth process required to "actively seek the wide, deep, and thoughtful engagement with high-quality literary and informational text that builds knowledge, enlarges experiences, and broadens worldviews" (Common Core State Standards Initiative, 2010, p. 3). As part of our modeling, we invite students to try the strategies we use. As they do, we remind them to return to the text as part of their discussions. With practice, they learn to read texts deeply in this way.

Of course, students also have to write about texts. After her class read Act 2, Scene 2 (the balcony scene), Ms. Lin asked the students to write poems in AABB quatrains that demonstrated their understanding of either Romeo or Juliet's character thus far in the play. Here is Juan's poem (used with permission), which he wrote and edited during the class period.

I Believe . . .

I believe that the sun shines after the rain
I believe in not making the same mistake again
I believe in not doing things the easy way
I believe that being selfish doesn't pay

I believe in a second chance
I believe in a life of long romance
I believe that first impressions last
I believe there is nothing better than a good laugh

I believe that dreams do come true
I believe there is destiny for me and you
I believe that good things come to those who wait
I believe love never arrives too late

I believe sometimes there is no explanation
I believe money can't buy affection
I believe you don't know what you've got until it's gone
I believe a new day arrives with every dawn

I believe in living life with no regrets
I believe that is as good as it gets
I believe the whole world is a stage
I believe we only get better with age

I believe we should look on the bright side
I believe that life is one big ride
I believe when I die people will grieve
But it's okay because I believe

Juan makes a number of connections between the text and his own life, but he can defend each of the lines in his poem as having a basis in the play. With intentional instruction and teacher modeling, reading like a detective becomes part of the critical reading habits of Juan, Allison, and their classmates as they read, connect with, and converse about a piece of literature.

Literature's Ability to Transform

The most obvious question to ask at this point is "Why read literature?" We are partial to Cullinan's (1989) explanation: literature provides both a window into and a mirror of the world. Through literature, readers meet people they might never have met and travel to places they may never visit. These windows allow students to peer inside possible worlds and consider the many ways other people live. Who can forget their first trip to Hogwarts School of Witchcraft and Wizardry (Rowling, 1997)? And how could we not have Old Yeller (Gipson, 1956/1995) in our lives? The Common Core State Standards also reflect this view of literature, highlighting the importance of having elementary students read literature to understand cultures. Likewise, the secondary standards discuss the need for students to read texts "across genres, cultures, and centuries" (Common Core State Standards Initiative, 2010, p. 35).

In addition to using literature as a window, readers see themselves in narrative texts—the mirror metaphor. Literature gives readers an opportunity to reflect on their own lives, and in the process validate and affirm their experiences with the world. Students often ask us, "Do you know of a book about . . . ?" The topic is usually predictable, based on what we know about the student. Take, for example, tenth-grader Mario, who was teased in middle school but is popular in high school. He likes to read about kids who are teased and what happens to them. When he found *Shattering Glass* (Giles, 2002), he couldn't stop talking about it. Similarly, when someone introduced him to *The Misfits* (Howe, 2001), he was ecstatic. At one point Mario said, "I finally get it. Everyone can be teased about something. It's just not fair. It doesn't have to be like that."

We'd like to add a third metaphor to Cullinan's (1989) description. Sometimes, literature is a door through which the reader walks, changed forever by the experience. These literary doors often open at developmentally significant times in the reader's life. Accessing this doorway function is an essential part of what deep reading of a text can do, because the transformative potential of a text might not be realized in one reading. It also requires matching the reader to the text.

While developmental theories abound, we have found Egan's (1997) framework of development especially instructive for teachers. He notes that "all educational theories involve people recapitulating, repeating for themselves, the discoveries and inventions that have accumulated through the history of their culture" (p. 27). For example, a young child learns to read for herself, going through processes similar to those that emerged six thousand years ago. Egan states that children move through a series of understandings that need to be satisfied before moving on to the next stage. Children in elementary school seek to answer the question, "Who am I?" This drives their reading as they eagerly consume information about their bodies and their communities. Young children learn the features of stories in order to tell the story of themselves.

Having sufficiently satisfied this question, children in the intermediate and middle grades are moved to explore a second understanding: "How big is the world?" They take in the broad measures of the physical, social, and biological worlds. What's the highest place on Earth? Who makes the rules for a country? How old can a person live to be? It is little wonder that books like *The Guinness Book of World Records* and *The Dangerous Book for Boys* (Iggulden & Iggulden, 2007) top the best-seller lists. Children in these grades are likely to view as purposeful and relevant any learning experiences that are designed to allow them to explore the limits of their world.

Having arrived at initial understandings about themselves and their world, adolescents seek to answer a third question: "Where do I fit into the world?" Exploration of self-identity is a hallmark of adolescence, and the seemingly bewildering shifts in persona make more sense when considered from this vantage point. In some ways, the struggle to answer this question is a consolidation of the first two understandings, and teenagers are quick to respond to topics that allow them to try on ideas as they sort out their positions and values. Educators sensitive to these needs structure their classrooms and readings in such a way that their students can chew on difficult or ambiguous concepts that require them to hold more than one viewpoint in their heads.

Of course, students don't arrive at our classroom doors quick to announce where they fall on the developmental continuum. In any classroom, you'll find students scattered across the spectrum. Personal experiences and individual strengths have a strong influence on students' cognitive curiosity. Regardless, for students to use literature to answer the big questions in their lives, they need to understand how literature works.

How Literature Works

Literature offers readers several significant features that they can use to make sense of what they read. We explore these components in the following sections and then turn our attention to the ways in which students can learn to read like detectives, comprehending, analyzing, and discussing texts.

Genre

There are a number of "types" of literature, each distinguished by specific characteristics. For example, fables are typically short stories in which animals or inanimate objects are given human qualities so that a moral is learned. Fables differ from other types of short stories because they are intended to teach the reader a lesson. When students understand the specific genre they are reading, they learn to anticipate the actions of the author and how the text will be constructed. At the most basic level, readers should recognize whether they are reading fiction (narrative literature) or nonfiction (expository literature). As they learn more about genre, students should be able to distinguish subtleties such as the difference between historical fiction and realistic fiction. We have found it useful to create broader categories of genres and then teach students about the different types of each text in each category. The genre wheel (fig. 3.1, page 54) is a helpful graphic for communicating these relationships to students.

Character

While plots are important, you couldn't really have a story without characters. The characters interact with one another to move the story along. As readers, we notice what the characters do and say, and we compare that with our own perspectives. Readers can learn about the characters a number of ways, including analyzing physical traits, dialogue, actions, attire, opinions, and points of view. Character analysis provides students with skills to evaluate external traits (for example, appearance or actions) and internal traits (for example, feelings or relationships). Sometimes, a narrator provides additional insight into the characters. An important consideration, and one that might be missed when students fail to return to the text and carefully analyze the author's words, is the emotions that the characters display. In their analysis of literature, Roser, Martinez, Yokota, and O'Neal (2005) suggest that character study is key to meaning making. In their words:

> As characters pull students into and through books, they stretch students' perspectives; they help them live out adventure and drama and conflict at a safe distance. Characters make the roadway seem traversable. They make plot comprehensible (and manageable). Characters lead students to deep, satisfying, and meaningful experiences with literature. In fact, students become more insightful about the human experience through the characters who tussle with crucial moral and ethical dilemmas. (p. vi)

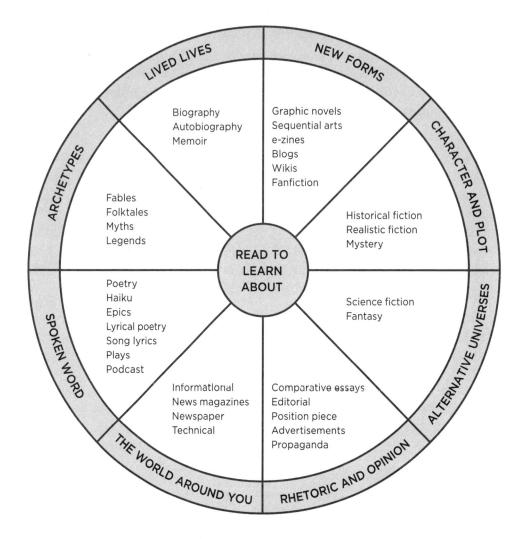

Source: Fisher & Frey (2009). Used with permission.

Figure 3.1: Genre wheel.

Dialogue

One of the ways that readers develop their understanding of characters, plot, and setting is through the dialogue that occurs between and among the characters. Of course, students must understand the punctuation marks that indicate dialogue, but they need to know more than that. To be fluent readers of literature, students have to practically hear the characters speak to them. The dialogue should trigger mental images—visualizations, if you will—of conversations between the characters. Often, it is the dialogue that provides insight into character motivation and feelings. As the literature that students read becomes increasingly complex, actions and emotions are implied by the author and inferred by the reader. These elements are not so blatantly stated, as they are in chapter books and young adult fiction.

Plot

Stories are plot driven. The plot includes all of the events that occur, including those that lead to the climax or conflict and those that allow for resolution. Combined with the setting, the plot draws the reader into the characters' lives and allows the reader to analyze their actions. In the 19th century, Gustav Freytag identified five specific components of the plot, which he diagrammed as a pyramid (fig. 3.2, page 56):

1. **Exposition.** Exposition is one of the rhetorical modes (along with argumentation, description, and narration) and is useful in providing the reader with the necessary background information. It is the beginning of the story, in which the characters and setting are first introduced. When readers miss the exposition or move their analysis too far away from the text early on, they are at increased risk for missing the point and failing to deeply understand the reading.

2. **Rising action.** The rising action includes all of the events leading up to the conflict. During rising action, characters interact, and the story moves forward. Readers who are in tune with the text realize that these events are leading up to a significant conflict or climax.

3. **Conflict.** In literature, a major conflict is typically identifiable in the rising action. Conflict is the struggle between opposing forces that grounds the story. It leads to the climax, as identified on the Freytag model. Quiller-Couch (1918) was the first to identify specific conflicts. He suggested that there were seven basic conflicts: man against man, man against nature, man against himself, man against god, man against society, man caught in the middle, and man against woman. This list of conflicts has been updated and revised over the years, and many such formulas now exist, such as individual versus self, individual versus individual, individual versus society, individual versus nature, individual versus supernatural, individual versus machine or technology, and individual versus destiny.

4. **Climax.** This is the high point of the story, in which the events peak. Often, the climax reveals secrets and missing details, and the conflict becomes clear. This revelation doesn't mean that climax is the most important part of the story, but rather that the reader now has the information necessary to predict how the characters will respond.

5. **Falling action.** This is the part of the story that occurs after the climax. Falling action focuses on the results and how the characters react to the climax. It can also include changes in the setting and often contains additional events that add clarity to the story.

6. **Resolution.** Although not all stories have a resolution, when they do, the resolution serves to tie up the loose ends and relieve the reader of tension and anxiety. In many books, the resolution is seen as cathartic.

Unfortunately, the resolution phase is a high-risk time for readers, especially those who disagree with the characters' actions. In many cases, students takes their own journey, neglecting to understand the ways in which the characters resolve the conflict and instead focusing on how they personally would have reacted. In these cases, readers miss valuable lessons and lose the opportunity to use literature as a window or door.

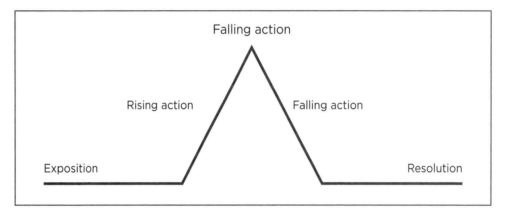

Source: Frey & Fisher (2006). Used with permission.

Figure 3.2: Freytag's pyramid.

Setting

Stories have to take place somewhere, and that somewhere is important. When readers understand the setting, including both the time and the location for the events that unfold, they can sometimes analyze the moods and motivations of various characters. Knowing, for example, the difference between the impact of a rural versus an urban environment, and between the years 1900 and 2000, will help readers determine if the actions and reactions of the characters coincide with that setting and with their own experiences, both direct and indirect. Again, when readers fail to understand the impact of the setting, they get lost in their own world and fail to recognize the significance of the world the author is creating.

Literary Devices

Authors of narrative texts often use specific literary devices to tell their story. They use them to describe, compare, and teach. In fact, it is the expert use of literary devices that makes some writing truly artistic. The Common Core State Standards address literary devices within the category of craft and structure. When students miss these devices, they miss significant parts of the storytelling. For example, as readers move from their early reading to classic and contemporary fiction, many of them miss the information implied in flashbacks. They become confused with the time shifts in novels and may even give up reading fiction altogether. When students notice and use literary devices to make meaning, they gain a deeper sense of the story and why the characters behave and think as they do.

Figure 3.3 contains a list of common literary devices. We should note that literary devices are also present in informational texts; however, teachers frequently teach about them using narrative text structures first. The list in figure 3.3 is not exhaustive; authors use many other literary devices to weave their stories.

Allegory. An allegory is a story that is used to teach something. Usually the stories are long and require analysis to find the allegory or intention. For example, the parables in the Bible and Aesop's fables are examples of allegories.

Alliteration. Alliteration occurs when the author uses the same letter or sound to start each word in a string. For example, "Andrea anxiously awaited arraignment." Alliteration is used frequently in books for emergent readers, in part to foster phonemic awareness.

Allusion. An allusion is a reference to a well-known person, myth, historical event, biblical story, and so on, as in "She's just like Narcissus" or "It's as bad as the sinking of the Titanic."

Flashback. A flashback pauses the action to comment or portray a scene that took place earlier. For example, during a scene in which a person walks through a dark alley, the author pauses to relate a story about another time the character was scared.

Foreshadowing. Foreshadowing is a hint of things to come—usually, but not always, an unpleasant event.

Hyperbole. Hyperbole is an exaggerated comment used for effect and not meant to be taken literally. For example, when faced with a long line at the Department of Motor Vehicles, Andrew said, "It will take an eternity to be allowed to drive."

Imagery. Imagery involves language that evokes one or all of the five senses—seeing, hearing, tasting, smelling, touching—as in "her lips taste of honey and dew" or "walking through the halls, amid the crashing sound of lockers closing and the smell of yesterday's coffee, I saw the radiant teacher."

Figure 3.3: Common literary devices.

(continued) →

Irony and satire. Irony and satire use sophisticated humor in relaying a message, often saying what something is when the opposite or reverse could be true. Authors use irony to say one thing when they mean another. For example, James is looking at the shark bite out of his surfboard and says, "Finally, I've got a short board." Satire focuses more on mockery or wit to attack or ridicule something.

Metaphor. In contrast with similes, metaphors make a direct statement and do not use "like" or "as" to make the comparison. Metaphors simply make a comparison in which one thing is said to be another. For example, "The dog's fur was electric, standing on end in fear."

Personification. When authors give animals, ideas, or actions the qualities of humans, we call it personification. This is common in Disney films as well as in children's books. Personification is also used for more abstract ideas such as "Hate has you trapped in her arms."

Point of view. Stories are often told from a specific point of view. In first person, the story is told from the perspective of the narrator, and we readers cannot know or witness anything the narrator does not tell us. In second person, the narrator speaks directly to the reader, as in "You will likely know by now that Andre is a bad guy." Finally, in third person, the narrator is omniscient (all-knowing) and can convey different perspectives at different times.

Simile. A simile is a statement in which two things are compared with "like" or "as." For example, "Like a rain-filled cloud, Anna cried and cried when she learned of her lost fortune."

Symbolism. When an object or action that means something more than its literal meaning is used, we note the symbolism. For example, when an author introduces a black crow into the text, readers are prepared for death. This compares with the sighting of a white dove, which conveys peace or life to readers.

Tone and mood. The attitude an author takes toward a subject or character, such as hateful, serious, humorous, sarcastic, solemn, or objective, conveys the tone or mood. The author can use dialogue, settings, or descriptions to set a tone or mood.

Source: Frey & Fisher (2006). Used with permission.

Illustrations

Although not all narrative texts contain illustrations, many do. Illustrations are not limited to picture books for young children; they also are common in graphic novels and other forms of sequential art. Now illustrations are appearing in narrative texts for older readers. For example, *Diary of a Wimpy Kid* (Kinney, 2007) and *The Curious Incident of the Dog in the Night-Time* (Haddon, 2003) would be markedly different books without their illustrations. When illustrations are included, they are a powerful support for student comprehension. As Sipe (2000) has demonstrated, the pictures are not there just for student enjoyment and motivation; they're also part of the reading and thinking process. In fact, Dyson (2006) advocates that teachers' everyday literacy instruction take advantage of students' engagement with visuals because of how significantly visuals influence one's linguistic and cultural experiences. Realizing that "the world told" differs so vastly from "the world shown" (Kress, 2003, p. 1), we believe that our goal of teaching students to interpret the text while interrogating the author's message should extend to their reading of visuals. We must teach that visuals share messages, which are depicted by how the message is displayed (space, colors, placement of objects, and so on), as well as what is displayed. Being able to understand the message embedded in a visual is referred to as *reading the grammar of the text* (Kress & van Leeuwen, 1996/2006). As we suggest later in this chapter and illustrate in chapter 5, being critically literate in the 21st century involves reading new-media texts that contain a new language structure that is rich with visuals (Albers, 2007).

Critical Literacy

Learners need to be able to analyze texts and their illustrations for their messages and structural elements, such as plot, theme, and character. But, as we have noted, in order to truly understand a book, readers must move beyond the New Critical theory of the mid-20th century and its deliberate rejection of anything beyond the text itself. In a critical literacy approach, readers consider themselves and the world around them in order to make judgments, ask larger questions, and contextualize the story.

Critical literacy is the practice of evaluating information, insights, and perspectives through an analysis of power, culture, class, and gender. To be critically literate, readers must come to understand that texts are not "true" but rather represent the perspectives of the writer and the sociocultural times in which they were written. The process of preparing critically literate readers provides students and teachers with a forum to analyze their varying topical perspectives while promoting increased student engagement and learning (Stevens & Bean, 2007).

Researchers and educators in Australia and New Zealand, who believed that literacy should be more than a one-way consumption of information, led the shift to a critical-literacy approach. The Tasmania (Australia) Department of Education further codified this approach by interjecting three overarching questions into the state's curricula:

1. In whose interest?
2. For what purpose?
3. Who benefits? (Tasmania Department of Education, 2007)

These questions not only echo Bean, Chappell, and Gillam's (2011) questions regarding purpose, audience, and genre (discussed in chapter 2), but push beyond them. A critical literacy stance invites students to look past the story itself to consider what is present and what has been left out. It seeks to locate bias, acknowledging that all texts possess a necessary viewpoint that highlights one view while shadowing another. We ask students in our classes to work regularly with four recurring themes:

1. Question the Commonplace in a Text
2. Consider the Role of the Author
3. Seek Alternative Perspectives
4. Read Critically (Frey, Fisher, & Berkin, 2008, p. 111)

We regard these themes as the keys to accessing information in a thoughtful and informed way. By constantly challenging students to take these elements into consideration, we hope to build habits of mind that will serve them long after they leave our classrooms. Our own practices and those of our colleagues confirm what we imagine many of you have also discovered in your work with adolescents: they love a good debate. In our efforts to teach argumentation (not arguing), we deliberately offer them texts that ask questions without furnishing the answers. We want to foster a healthy skepticism balanced by deep knowledge and a desire to always ask, "What if?" For us, the ability to ask these questions, seek out answers, and form judgments lies at the heart of literacy.

Question the Commonplace

The world of literature is full of archetypes that provide opportunities to question assumptions about power, race, class, and gender. Princesses are always delicate and fairly helpless, unless you're talking about Elizabeth in *The Paper Bag Princess* (Munsch, 1992). The many versions of *The Ugly Duckling* can give rise to discussions about conventional definitions of beauty, especially when paired with Cinderella stories such as *The Rough-Face Girl* (Martin, 1998). First-grade teacher Ryan Bourke (2008) described how he used fairy tales like *Jack and the Beanstalk* to raise questions about rules and *The Three Billy Goats Gruff* to challenge how power is misused. Students discussed these issues and wrote their own versions of the stories. Burke noted:

> When my students were granted agency to adjust factions of power, their fairy tale renditions resonated with evidence of critical thinking—thinking that was extended to other areas of the curriculum. As we read other genres, my students transferred their critical skills and began to discern the inequities present in various text types, deconstructing them in their conversations and writing. (p. 311)

But critical literacy should not be limited to printed texts. We can extend the practices of critical literacy to students' oral language development through discussion. This approach is especially important for English learners and speakers of African American Vernacular English, who often feel marginalized during language arts instruction and leave the experience thinking that their home language is not good enough (Labov, 1995; Ogbu, 2003). The critical literacy stance has allowed Diane to challenge this assumption and provide instruction to her students in ways that validate their home languages and extend their understanding of other language registers.

During the 2008 presidential campaign, many of Diane's students told her that they believed Barack Obama would win the election because "he could talk to everyone."

CHARLES: Obama probably only talks black at home.

LEVON: True that. He knows when he can be talking like a homie.

DAVEON: His mom family was white.

CHARICE: You can talk like that even when you black.

DAVEON: Can you?

CHARLES: I want to.

Diane leveraged the students' interest in current events and their own linguistic backgrounds as English learners or speakers of African American Vernacular English to launch an exploration of language registers. The students read and discussed a letter written by Henry Louis Gates, Jr., to the editor of the *New York Times* and the responses it received. They examined the use of dialect in the writings of Samuel Clemens (Mark Twain) and debated the reasons why *The Adventures of Huckleberry Finn* (1885/2001) is often challenged for its language. The students' close interrogation of the uses of language registers and the assumptions of power, class, and race that are represented provided an important background for understanding the presidential campaign of 2008.

Consider the Role of the Author

Fiction is often written in the style of a memoir, using a first-person narrator. The narrator may be an unreliable one, as in many of Edgar Allan Poe's short stories, or may possess a narrow perspective that limits his or her ability to fully understand what is happening. For instance, in *The Music of the Dolphins* (Hesse, 1998), Mila is a child who has been raised by dolphins but now finds herself "rescued" by well-meaning but intrusive scientists. Her limited understanding of language and the world around her is reflected in the strained syntax: "I like good," she says in the first chapter (p. 8). Although Mila gains knowledge of the human world, it is not without sorrow, sparking much discussion among elementary and middle school students about the wisdom of such interference.

Students can also gain a deeper understanding of a fictional work by knowing more about the person who wrote it. The seventh-grade students in Ms. Fontaine's English class examined the importance of the immigration experience for author An Na and the protagonist of her novel *A Step From Heaven* (2002). The story is set in San Diego, where Ms. Fontaine's students live as well. Although a work of fiction, the story was inspired by the author's memories of arriving from Korea as a four-year-old. The students read interviews with the author to glean connections between her experiences and those of the fictional Young Ju:

> **BRENT:** I read [in the interview] that she said she remembered getting a perm.
>
> **DAISHA:** They told her all Americans had curly hair . . .
>
> **BRENT:** . . . but on her first day of school, she found out they didn't.
>
> **AMIRA:** It's on page 31. (Reads) "I see some girls whispering to each other. I have never seen so many different colors of hair." Then she counts the number of kids with black hair—"night hair" like her. (Reads) "But not all the Americans have curly hair like Gomo said they would. Only one boy has big curly hair. I hope they do not think I am a boy."
>
> **FATHIA:** I remember what it was like when I first got here from Somalia. There wasn't anything that seemed familiar.
>
> **DAISHA:** Korea, that's where she [the author] is coming from. In that interview we read, she talked about locking herself in the bathroom at home to read because that was the only room in the house with a lock on it.
>
> **BRENT:** Yeah, she sounded pretty lonely.
>
> **FATHIA:** That's what Young Ju was feeling, too. There wasn't anyone she could talk to. Her parents didn't understand what was happening at school, and there wasn't anyone at school to talk about being Korean.
>
> **AMIRA:** Remember in the interview, she [the author] talked about fights at home with her parents for the same reason?

The students in this group are moving smoothly back and forth between two texts to make connections between the author's lived experiences and those of her fictional counterpart. Importantly, each text enriches the students' understanding of the other.

Seek Alternative Perspectives

F. Scott Fitzgerald once wrote that "the test of a first-rate intelligence is the ability to hold two opposed ideas in the mind at the same time and still retain the ability to function" (1945, p. 69). In order for students to do so, they need to read and discuss how one's point of view shifts depending on the perspective. For example, students can read graphic novel pairs that offer two perspectives on a similar topic. Eric Heuvel's books *A Family Secret* (2009a) and *The Search* (2009b) tell the fictional stories of Esther and Helena, two girls growing up in the Netherlands during World War II. What is not clear is whether Helena's family betrayed Esther's to the Nazis in order to survive. Each book is told through flashback as the women recount the tales to their grandchildren, and only at the end of the second book is it clear what really occurred.

Another graphic novel plays out two points of view simultaneously. Lemke's (2010) series *Good Vs. Evil* uses red and blue paths on the same page so that the reader can follow the storyline of the protagonist or the antagonist. In *Awakening*, the first graphic novel in the series, the reader can see the plot unfolding in real time as a young teen plays a cassette tape of music he has found, only to awaken a monster in the sewers below.

Young readers take delight in finding out the other side of the story. Ms. Adams used two books with her kindergarten students as shared reading experiences. The first was *The True Story of the Three Little Pigs* (Sciezka, 1996), which is attributed to "A. Wolf" and recounts the infamous tale from his perspective. He claims he was only going from house to house to borrow sugar but unfortunately kept sneezing due to a bad cold. The students acted out each version of the story using a Reader's Theater approach with Ms. Adams serving as the narrator.

The second book was *Dear Mrs. La Rue: Letters From Obedience School* (Teague, 2002). This book engaged the students with its split-page illustrations depicting the reality of naughty dog Ike's experiences and his exaggerated letters to his owner, all filled with doom and gloom. The students were struck by one paired illustration in particular, of Ike dining in a fine restaurant (reality) and a contrasting picture of him in striped prison clothes, holding out a tin cup to receive a ladle of food from an intimidating cook:

MS. ADAMS:	Let's look closely at this picture. What do they have in common?
PHILIP:	Ike is getting something to eat.
MS. ADAMS:	But what's different about the two?
JOANNA:	(pointing to the restaurant scene) He's got a dog treat in his hand!
RANDALL:	My dog likes treats.
PHILIP:	And he has a napkin 'round his neck, like when you eat lobster.
RANDALL:	Look at the waiter guy. He has that plate and the cover. The silver cover. Like you lift it.

JOANNA:	For something fancy.
MS. ADAMS:	And what's happening here? (points to the prison scene)
PHILIP:	He looks scared.
LUCAS:	The big guy is scary.
MS. ADAMS:	The sign he's pointing to says, "No howling, biting, scratching, growling, slobbering, or barking and no seconds!"
RANDALL:	No treats for Ike (makes a dramatically sad face).
MS. ADAMS:	Do you believe he is telling the truth in his letter to Mrs. La Rue? He says, "Were the neighbors really complaining that much about my barking? It is hard to imagine. First, I didn't bark that much. You were away those nights, so you wouldn't know, but trust me, it was quite moderate." That means he only barked a little bit. What do you think?
JOANNA:	No, he's telling a fib! He prob'ly barked lots.
MS. ADAMS:	What helps you decide that?
JOANNA:	'Cause he's not telling her the truth 'bout his eating.
RANDALL:	He makes it sound real bad, like he doesn't get good food.
LUCAS:	But he does for real.
PHILIP:	I think he barked lots. Like woofwoofwoofwoofwoofwoof!
JOANNA:	(covering her ears in mock discomfort) Stop it! You're hurting my ears!
LUCAS:	That's what the neighbors said! (All the children cover their ears and begin protesting.)

Although critical literacy is often portrayed as taking a serious approach to the text, clearly Ms. Adams chose to use her students' sense of humor to get them to contrast opposing viewpoints. Their appreciation for humor served as a natural pathway for them to examine how the main character exploited a skewed perspective for his own gain.

Read Critically

As an astute reader, you pick up a book or short story and almost immediately begin asking questions of the text. You search for the time and location, knowing that the setting will help you glean some insight into the story. You question the motives of the characters, wondering what human foibles will be exposed through their thoughts and actions. In other words, you expect that the story you are told is probably not going to be the only story. The reader who looks beyond the literal meaning will find another layer of meaning. You know that your view as a reader, often aided by an omniscient narrator, makes you privy to understanding events in ways the characters cannot.

Or perhaps not. The unreliable narrator introduces a further need to read critically. The series written by Lemony Snicket, starting with *The Bad Beginning* (1999), introduces us to a snide and not altogether benign narrator, much to the delight of young readers who know they must look beyond the story's events to understand just how much danger the Baudelaire children are really in. Likewise, Reynie, Kate, Sticky, and Constance, the sleuths in *The Mysterious Benedict Society* (Stewart, 2008) face both the mysteries of defeating a villain and a narrator who holds back information that could help the children and the reader. The master of the unreliable narrator is Edgar Allan Poe, whose short stories are memorable for vivid and suspect narrators who cannot be trusted to give the reader an unbiased account of the proceedings.

Mysteries are a natural for reading critically to unearth clues and solve puzzles. *The Calder Game* (Balliett, 2010) is ideal for students to read closely in order to solve an art crime: a mobile by Alexander Calder goes missing. The author's website (www. scholastic.com/blueballiett) provides additional short puzzles related to this book. One activity allows readers to create a series of newspaper accounts of a stolen work of art of their choice, the investigation of the crime, and the solution. Mysteries like this and many others invite students to read closely and critically so as not to miss a single important detail.

In order to have discussions similar to those we've shared here, students need opportunities and reasons to consult the text. Fortunately, teachers can use a number of instructional routines that support the reading of a wide array of literature, including read-alouds, shared reading, book clubs, and collaborative conversations.

Useful Instructional Routines for Text-Based Analysis and Discussion

Being able to participate fully in a text-based literature discussion requires that students realize the expectations for doing so and the behaviors that support their participatory success. Teachers and students should determine what is expected of each student as he or she works with others, what behaviors the group deems acceptable, and what expectations students can have of others in their shared community of learners. The routines, or sets of procedures, we share in this section are designed to enable students to become independent learners who have the skills needed to take responsibility for both seeking and sharing information.

Thinking Aloud Through Read-Alouds and Shared Readings

Thinking aloud allows students to experience the cognitive processes of an expert. Teachers can engage students in a think-aloud in a number of ways, and they can use this process for both narrative and expository texts. When the think-aloud is focused on texts, the teacher can use two common processes: read-alouds and shared readings.

Read-alouds and shared readings enable teachers to help students learn to return to the text as they talk about or write about what they are reading. Typically, in a read-aloud, the teacher reads the text, sharing his or her thinking with students. The text selected for a read-aloud is usually above the instructional level of the average student in the class because the teacher provides the necessary scaffolds for students to understand the text. The students do not see the text, but they may have opportunities to see the illustrations or other visual information. Read-alouds are a powerful way to build students' background knowledge and vocabulary. In a study of highly effective teacher read-alouds (Fisher, Flood, Lapp, & Frey, 2004), we identified seven essential components that led to success:

1. Books chosen were appropriate to students' interests and matched to their developmental, emotional, and social levels.
2. Selections had been previewed and practiced by the teacher.
3. A clear purpose for the read-aloud was established.
4. Teachers modeled fluent oral reading when they read the text.
5. Teachers were animated and used expression.
6. Teachers stopped periodically and thoughtfully questioned the students to focus them on specifics of the text.
7. Connections were made to independent reading and writing. (pp. 10–11)

Shared readings have some things in common with read-alouds, namely that the teacher is the reader and shares his or her thinking aloud with students while reading. But shared readings differ from read-alouds in that the students can see the text as the teacher reads it. This means that the selected text is easier to read—it is probably at or below the instructional level and often at the independent level—because students are reading along with the teacher. During shared readings, teachers often model their understanding in four ways: comprehension, word solving, text structures, and text features (Fisher, Frey, & Lapp, 2008b).

Fifth-grade teacher Sandy Rutherford modeled her understanding using a think-aloud process (Davey, 1983; described in chapter 2) as she conducted a shared reading of *Moon Over Manifest* (Vanderpool, 2010). She paused at the term *speakeasy*, saying, "I've seen that word before, and I remembered that it's two words put together, to remind a person to whisper. That helps me remember that a speakeasy is a place where they sold illegal alcohol, so they wanted everyone to keep it a secret." A few pages later, Ms. Rutherford paused after reading a passage about the protagonist repeatedly flipping a coin to make a decision. "Boy, I've done that before, when I wanted the answer to be 'no' so I could avoid doing something. And just like Abilene, when I didn't get the answer I wanted, I flipped the coin again. That makes me think that she really doesn't want to go inside the psychic's house." Think-alouds like this one afford students the opportunity to see how an expert reader returns to the text to more fully understand what is happening in the book.

Book Clubs and Literature Circles

Book clubs and literature circles are also useful for teaching students to return to the text during discussions (Daniels, 2002; Raphael, Florio-Ruane, & George, 2001). In general, students working in book clubs or literature circles read a book in common and then meet to discuss the text they're reading. That doesn't mean that all of the groups are reading the same book, but rather that all members of the group are reading the same book.

Book clubs and literature circles differ in some ways, mainly with regard to the formality of the processes used. In book clubs, students typically participate in four components: community share, reading, writing/representing, and book club discussion. During the community share, the teacher provides instruction, and the students participate in discussions with the entire class. In a book club, there is also time dedicated to reading, which is typically done individually. During the writing and representing phase, students, who often select their own books (Lapp & Fisher, 2009b), reflect on what they have read, either in writing such as journal entries or through an artistic response such as an illustration or poem. The fourth component of a book club focuses on the small-group discussion that students reading the same book have with one another.

In contrast, literature circles are more informal. Daniels (1994) identifies twelve key features of literature circles, each of which is useful in establishing and operating these groups:

1. Students *choose* their own reading materials.
2. *Small temporary groups* are formed, based on book choice.
3. Different groups read *different books*.
4. Groups meet on a *regular, predictable schedule* to discuss their reading.
5. Kids use written or drawn *notes* to guide both their reading and discussion.
6. Discussion *topics come from the students*.
7. Group meetings aim to be *open, natural conversations about books* so personal connections, digressions, and open-ended questions are welcome.
8. In newly forming groups, students play a rotating assortment of task *roles*.
9. The teacher serves as a *facilitator*, not group member or instructor.
10. Evaluation is by *teacher observation and student self-evaluation*.
11. A spirit of *playfulness and fun* pervades the room.
12. When books are finished, *readers share with their classmates*, and the *new groups form* around new reading choices. (p. 18, emphasis in original)

In terms of our discussion here, feature number seven is important. Students should be encouraged to make personal connections and digressions, but we would add that their conversations should return to the text regularly to determine the author's purpose and perspective. Again, that's not to say that students spend their entire time analyzing what the author said, but rather that they base their conversations on the words in the text.

Task roles are an important part of literature circles, especially as new groups form. Students can assume a number of different roles, depending on the purpose for reading the text and how many students are in the group. For example, a group might need a discussion director who keeps the conversation moving. Students might also act as illustrators, connectors, or summarizers or serve in a variety of other roles (for information on specific roles, see www.edselect.com/literature_circles.htm). Importantly, these roles serve as a temporary scaffold until the group members gain confidence in their ability to talk deeply about a text, and they should be phased out to allow more natural conversations to emerge. The key to the use of literature circles and book clubs, however, is that students learn how to have conversations that regularly return to the text.

We've found it helpful to have an essential question guide the book club selections so that students can talk together in a large-group format and contribute their perspectives on the question, as informed by the book they are reading. For example, when eleventh-grade students were focused on the essential question, "Can you buy your way to happiness?" they selected books to read and then met in groups to discuss them. One of the groups read *Feed* (Anderson, 2004), while another group read *The Great Gatsby* (Fitzgerald, 1925), and another group read *So Yesterday* (Westerfeld, 2004). When the students met in their book clubs, they discussed the essential question and their own perspectives on the books. As part of their conversation, they regularly returned to the text to directly quote what the author said and then debate the meaning of the quote. During a discussion focused on chapter 3 of *The Great Gatsby*, the students in that book club contributed the following:

MICHAEL: They sure drink a lot in this book. I mean, they seem to like to get drunk.

EDITH: I agree. Like when the guy with the big glasses is sitting at the table talking.

REBECCA: But that's not the point of the chapter, right? I mean he's trying to tell us something else.

MICHAEL: Yeah, you're right. I was just surprised about how much they drink in this book!

REBECCA: So, what is the key idea from this chapter?

EDITH: I think we're getting to know Gatsby a bit better. He's not doing what the other people are doing. He doesn't drink or dance; he just watches.

MICHAEL: But he sure has a lot of money. Maybe he buys happiness with his money this way—to have parties for people so that he can think he has friends.

REBECCA: So, he's obviously rich. They even say that he has real books, as if that makes a person rich.

EDITH: But maybe back then everyone didn't have books at home. My grandma always talks about going to the library to get books, ten at a time, because they didn't own any at her house.

MICHAEL: So, again, it's about how much money he has, but is he happy? We don't know yet.

One way that Edith responded to the essential question was to write the following poem (used with permission). Edith struggles with school, in terms of both attendance and achievement, but she says that she enjoys the book clubs and literature circles because she "gets to hear what other people think" and then compare that with her own ideas.

Money Isn't Everything . . .

It can buy a bed—but not sleep

It can buy a clock—but not time

It can buy a book—but not knowledge

It can buy a position—but not respect

It can buy medicine—but not health

It can buy blood—but not life

It can buy sex—but not love

So you see, money isn't everything, and it often causes pain and suffering. I tell you all this because I am your friend, and as your friend I want to take away your pain and suffering . . . So send me all your money and I will suffer for you!

Dialectical Journals

A chief goal in text-based discussions is getting students to return to the text. A *dialectical journal* invites students to read closely for passages that inspire or confound. The journal page is split into two columns: students write direct quotes from the text on the left as they read, then comment on the quotes on the right. These comments may include reactions to and analyses of the text. These double-entry journals are designed to encourage readers to notice how their thinking evolves as they move through a story. A simple format for younger students, as shown in figure 3.4, may include prompts that alert them to the type of writing they are examining. The template asks students to cite specific, memorable lines, or "Golden Lines," that provide the requested information, and to record their impressions.

What are you reading? _____	
Golden Lines and Page Number	**What I Thought About as I Read It**
A quote from a character	
A choice a character had to make	
Another character's reaction to the choice	

Figure 3.4: Dialectical journal format for younger readers.

Older students can analyze and reflect on passages in more detail but also benefit from a format that guides their close reading. We like the approach Calkins (1994) suggests for using dialectical journals (she calls them *double-entry ledgers*) as a means for spurring discussion. She advises that students record their reflections and analyses both before and after discussion so that they can witness how their thinking about the text has been shaped by conversation.

In addition, this approach provides students with a scaffold to identify specific places in the text that lend themselves to rich discussion. Consider a journal entry Susana wrote as she read the first chapter of *Thirteen Reasons Why* (Asher, 2007). Susana knows the basic outline of the story: a teenage girl commits suicide and leaves cassette tapes detailing the thirteen reasons why she did so. Susana's dialectical journal notes from chapter 1 (see the first two columns of fig. 3.5, page 71) will prepare her for the literature circle discussion she will have with several other students who are reading the same book.

Title of Book: <u>Thirteen Reasons Why</u>
Chapter/page numbers: <u>1/1–4</u> Date: <u>3/9</u>

Memorable Quotes	What I'm Thinking About as I Read It	After Discussion
"Baker's dozen," I mumble. Then I feel disgusted for even noticing it. (p. 1)	That word disgusted is ominous. Sounds like something evil will happen.	Foreshadowing
"You're missing a dollar." (p. 2)	Clay is distracted.	He says he's tired, but he's also troubled by the package.
"Did they keep their receipts as sick souvenirs?" (p. 3)	There's another hint that this will not be a happy story. Disgusted and sick both in the first chapter.	There's another hint a few paragraphs later, when Clay talks about his pounding headache and his fear that he'll collapse. Interesting word choices by the author.
"And in the middle of the room, one desk to the left, will be the desk of Hannah Baker. Empty." (p. 4)	There it is. I expected it, but now it's clear that the book is going to address the suicide from the beginning.	That one word all by itself at the very end of the first chapter just leaves you hanging, like you just fell off a cliff. Eduardo said it was like having a hole in your stomach.

Figure 3.5: Susana's journal entries.

Here is an excerpt from the students' discussion after Susana wrote her initial notes:

SUSANA: We know the book is about a suicide and the thirteen reasons why the girl said she did it, but I was surprised that he [the author] didn't waste any time.

JEFFREY: Yeah, he says about her desk being empty at school. It's on page four.

EDUARDO: And he [Clay] talks about dragging himself into the ivy that is on the sidewalk to school. I wrote that one down.

SUSANA: That's a good one.

EDUARDO: But that "empty" sentence. The last line of the chapter. It's like it gave me a feeling like I had a hole in my stomach.

JEFFREY: Like a hole in the classroom.

SUSANA: I think that's exactly what we're supposed to feel. Makes you want to read what's on the cassette.

The notes Susana made before the group met prepared her for the conversation, enabling her to recognize that the feeling of emptiness created by the author might compel a reader to find out what's going on. Her notes after the discussion, which appear in the third column of figure 3.5, suggest a deepening understanding of the opening structure of the book's first chapter. Susana identifies the literary device of foreshadowing, focuses on the author's word choice, and adopts Eduardo's idiomatic description of "a hole in your stomach."

Socratic Seminar

The Socratic seminar is a useful approach for discussing literature in a whole-class format. An effective seminar session typically lasts between thirty and fifty minutes and includes four major components: the text being considered, the questions raised, the seminar leader, and the participants. Importantly, a Socratic seminar is based on the text itself, and students are encouraged to refer back to it regularly. The seminar is not focused on memorizing the text, but rather on how to make an argument informed by the text.

Developing such an argument requires attention to the second component, the questions raised. The first question in a Socratic seminar is usually open ended, with no clear answer. This question should reflect interest and curiosity on the part of the leader as well as provide participants with an opportunity to return to the text as they consider, speculate, evaluate, analyze, define, and clarify the issues involved. Sample questions useful during a Socratic seminar include the following:

- **Sample questions to serve as the key question or interpret the text:**
  What is the main idea or underlying value in the text?
  What is the author's purpose or perspective?
  What does (a particular phrase) mean?
  What might be a good title for the text?
  What is the most important word/sentence/paragraph?

- **Sample questions to move the discussion along:**
  Who has a different perspective?
  Who has not yet had a chance to speak?
  Where do you find evidence for that in the text?
  Can you clarify what you mean by that?
  How does that relate to what (someone else) said?
  Is there something in the text that is unclear to you? Has anyone changed his or her mind? (Chowning & Fraser, 2007, p. 107)

	Exemplary	Proficient	Partially Proficient	Developing	Comments
Analysis and Reasoning	• Clearly references text to support reasoning. • Demonstrates thoughtful consideration of the topic. • Provides relevant and insightful comments; makes new connections. • Demonstrates exceptionally logical and organized thinking. • Moves the discussion to a deeper level.	• Occasionally references text to support reasoning. • Demonstrates consideration of the topic. • Provides relevant comments. • Displays thinking that is clear and organized.	• Rarely references text, may reference text incorrectly. • Demonstrates awareness of the topic but little reflection on it. • Comments are mostly relevant. • Displays thinking that is mostly clear and organized.	• Does not reference text. • Demonstrates little or no consideration of the topic. • Comments are off-topic or irrelevant. • Displays thinking that is confused, disorganized, or stays at a very superficial level.	
Discussion Skills	• Speaks loudly and clearly. • Stays on topic and brings discussion back on topic if necessary. • Talks directly to other students (rather than the teacher). • Stays focused on the discussion. • Invites other people into the discussion. • Shares "air time" equally with others. • References the remarks of others.	• Speaks at an appropriate level to be heard. • Stays on topic and focused on the discussion. • Is aware of sharing "air time" with others and may invite them into the conversation. • May occasionally direct comments to teacher.	• Mostly speaks at an appropriate level but may need to be coached. • Sometimes strays from topic. • Occasionally dominates the conversation.	• Cannot be heard, or may dominate the conversation. • Demonstrates inappropriate discussion skills.	

(continued) →

Figure 3.6: Socratic seminar rubric.

	Exemplary	Proficient	Partially Proficient	Developing	Comments
Clarity	• Listens to others respectfully by making eye contact with the speaker and waiting her turn to speak. • Makes remarks that are polite and demonstrate a high level of concern for the feelings of others. • Addresses others in a civil manner, using a collegial and friendly tone.	• Listens to others respectfully. • Uses appropriate language and tone. • Remarks demonstrate a concern for the feelings of others.	• Listens to others respectfully, but may not always look at the speaker or may sometimes interrupt. • Remarks demonstrate an awareness of feelings of others.	• May be distracted or not focused on the conversation. • Interrupts frequently. • Remarks demonstrate little awareness or sensitivity to the feelings of others. • Uses an aggressive, threatening, or otherwise inappropriate tone.	

Source: Rosetta Lee, Seattle Girls' School, Seattle, Washington. Used with permission.

The seminar leader, who is also a participant in the conversation, often poses these questions. At first, the seminar leader is probably the teacher. Over time, and with experience, students can assume the role of the seminar leader, and the teacher can become one of the participants.

The final component, the participants, is important because members of a Socratic seminar must come to the meeting prepared, meaning they have read the text and are ready to talk. The classroom climate and culture must allow participants to share their thinking and not be humiliated because of their ideas. To acquaint students with the norms for participation, teachers might show one of the short videos of Socratic seminars that are available on video-sharing sites such as TeacherTube and SchoolTube. Teachers can also use rubrics to guide student participation, through feedback, in these seminars. We particularly like the rubric created by Rosetta Lee (fig. 3.6, page 73), because it intentionally draws students back to the text and clearly requires that students refer to the text for support.

In the following excerpt from a Socratic seminar, notice how Javier Villanueva, as the discussion leader, gently encourages his tenth-grade students to support their thinking with text-based information. The students are reading *The Boy in the Striped Pajamas* (Boyne, 2007) as a part of their study of World War II.

MR. VILLANUEVA: When I was reading *The Boy in the Striped Pajamas,* I was thinking about the moral or the message the author was trying to share. Especially as I also thought about all that we have learned about what happened to Jewish people during World War II.

MARIA: I know. That's tricky to really decide.

STEVEN: Do you mean what the author wants us to gain or learn?

MR. VILLANUEVA: Yes, exactly.

SEYO: Treat each other with respect.

GENEMO: Yeah! No matter who you are or where you come from.

ANTHONY: Or what you look like.

MR. VILLANUEVA: Those are terrific possibilities. What made you think of them? Can you each find evidence in the text that moved you to think as you do?

ANTHONY: Well right here on page 128, Schmuel is talking about what it's like to live in his house.

GENEMO: Yeah, but remember it's not really a house.

STEVEN: That's right! They live in a concentration camp.

ANTHONY: And Schmuel is telling Bruno about how he gets hit "even when I did nothing wrong."

STEVEN: And later on that same page, it talks about all those people in the trains. It was so crowded and smelly for them!

MR. VILLANUEVA: So let's take what you are all saying and link it back to helping me understand the moral.

SEYO: That's about the author's message.

MR. VILLANUEVA: Yes!

MARIA: The author is writing about many times when the characters are not treated with respect. And these two examples tell us that there were unfair conditions for Schmuel and the others.

ANTHONY: That's right! Bruno wasn't living like those people with the striped pajamas in the concentration camp. It just wasn't right. It wasn't respectful.

MARIA: Once Bruno started to realize this, he also knew this was wrong.

SEYO: I think it ended they way it did to show that evil causes more evil. My dad says this happens with all wars.

MR. VILLANUEVA: That is great thinking. You sure used the text to illustrate your thoughts.

Mr. Villanueva's wondering and also asking for text support modeled for his students the recursive process that must occur as readers use their personal insights to gain meaning when reading and conversing about texts.

Modeling Inquiry for Students

Although students and teachers share a classroom learning community, the model of inquiry that the teacher presents needs to illustrate how to positively accept students' ideas and questions as well as how to explore them by investigating, navigating, and evaluating multiple sources of information. This inquisitive tone establishes an inquiry-based and reflective classroom atmosphere. Teachers convey the specifics of personal navigation by modeling how they view the thoughts and information presented by other members of the community, as well as those shared through multimodal sources. As the teacher models intellectual inquiry, students come to realize that to be critically literate does not mean to disrespect the thoughts of others. To the contrary, it means to contextually evaluate ideas in an attempt to fully comprehend them as a means to formulate a personal knowledge base. It is important that teachers model that this kind of evaluation is a positive way of interacting, since critically questioning a text or a person may seem to be contrary to what many children were taught about respecting others and not talking back.

Through modeling, teachers can show that intellectual curiosity is natural and that asking probing questions is a means to stimulate one's evaluative thinking. When teachers establish an atmosphere of inquiry, students are no longer anxious about admitting that they do not know something. Instead they see this admission as a jumping-off place for their inquiry.

Supporting Investigation of Multiple Perspectives

Outside of mathematics, few answers are set in stone. Teachers help students understand the importance of hosting multiple perspectives by gathering multiple texts with varying points of view on a topic and then modeling how to identify and compare these perspectives (Giorgis & Johnson, 2002). They question the texts (Raphael, 1986) while modeling how to compile insights about each author, including possible intent. Effective teachers also model how to contrast new and sometimes conflicting pieces of information with one's existing base of knowledge. Further, they model that it's important to evaluate each point of view within its sociocultural environment so that the thinker better understands other perspectives and expands his or her own. Our goal was to model how to garner multiple perspectives and then to evaluate the source, the speaker, and the intent of each, and additionally to support students as they "tried on" and determined the situational appropriateness of their thinking and language.

Conclusion

Our intent in this chapter has been to provide examples of instruction and instructional routines that give students opportunities to grow as readers who read "with a critical edge" (Pearson, 2001) as they challenge the text with insights from the world as they know it. We believe that the process of reading and knowing is recursive, because as one acquires new knowledge, the world, as previously perceived, changes. As we've discussed, to be able to read with a critical stance, one must examine, question, and argue (within a literary context) while considering the author's style and the intended message. To fully understand, the reader must contrast the derived message with his or her own base of knowledge, which results from insights gleaned from reading the thoughts of others and experiencing life within one's personal context. Our goal is similar to that of other educators who hope to instill in their students the power of knowing that they can envision perspectives other than those presented by the author and that they can use their own valued voices to share their understandings.

CHAPTER 4

Analyzing and Discussing Expository Texts

WHEN ANGELICA ASKED HER TEACHER for a book about stars, he asked, "What kind of stars? You know, that word has a lot of different meanings. Are you thinking about the night sky or famous people?" Angelica, who was used to her teacher's encouraging her to use specific terminology, responded, "I want to read more about celestial stars, like the ones in our textbook." Her teacher replied, "Oh, excellent. I think you'll find some very good information about these massive, luminous balls of plasma that are held together by gravity in this book," and he handed her *A Child's Introduction to the Night Sky* (Driscoll, 2004). "Wow, cool! Thanks!" Angelica exclaimed as she left her sixth-grade science class on her way to humanities.

When she got to her humanities class, her teacher, Mr. Ryan, noticed the book she was carrying and asked, "Did you pick that one? I didn't know you were into stars." Angelica replied, "I wasn't, until we read about these balls of plasma in the sky. Now I want to find out more and more. Why?" Mr. Ryan responded, "I think there's a book in here someplace about Tycho Brahe [Gow, 2002], the astronomer who built his own observatory way back in the 1500s, medieval times." Angelica, with a look of astonishment on her face, asked, "Really, they've been able to study stars, I mean plasma held together with gravity, for that long? Can you help me find that book?"

Expository, informational, nonfiction texts are interesting to students like Angelica, who all want to understand the world around them. While these texts are often considered harder than narrative texts, they are motivating for students. In this chapter, we'll explore the types of expository texts, why they are hard, and how students can learn to return to the text for evidence. If students are to reach high levels of success, such as those described in the Common Core State Standards, they must be able to read and think critically about what they read. Consider, for example, the key ideas and details of the reading standards for literacy in history/social studies:

1. Cite specific textual evidence to support analysis of primary and secondary sources.

2. Determine the central ideas or information of a primary or secondary source; provide an accurate summary of the source distinct from prior knowledge or opinions.

3. Identify key steps in a text's description of a process related to history/social studies (e.g., how a bill becomes law, how interest rates are raised or lowered). (Common Core State Standards Initiative, 2010, p. 61)

Expository Text Defined

Expository texts focus on the biological, social, and physical worlds around us (Fountas & Pinnell, 2001). They differ from fiction in accuracy and authority, although the degree of those qualities can be somewhat subjective, as some expository genres include editorial content. Moss (2003) calls expository texts "the literature of fact" and states that they "explain or inform" (p. 13). While narratives tell a story that comes primarily from the writer's imagination, expository texts provide explanations using information that can be corroborated by other sources. This is, of course, a somewhat squishy distinction, because genre-crossing forms exist. For example, a book of *Peanuts* cartoons may be autobiographical but more narrative in nature, while a biography of *Peanuts* creator Charles Schultz is informational. Another dichotomous set of descriptors is fiction and nonfiction, which further divides texts by the relative amount of factual, not imaginative, content.

Type (the format or method of manufacture) and *genre* (the content) provide further dimensions to the descriptions of expository texts. There are many types of expository text, such as newspapers, trade books, digital sources, picture books, photographic essays, and graphic novels, and all can be sources of information.

The purposes of expository texts may vary widely as well, and this influences the way the information is presented. *How-to* (procedural) texts are likely to be laid out sequentially, perhaps even numbered and accompanied by diagrams. *Definitional* texts, such as dictionaries and encyclopedias, are often used as references and are arranged alphabetically and/or by topic, while *descriptive* texts give extended examples to illustrate the topic or concept. This book is an example of an extended descriptive text. *Persuasive* pieces feature the elements of argumentation discussed in chapter 2 and include speeches, editorials, and opinion columns. The purpose of *analytical* texts is to delve deeply into a topic by examining each aspect of the topic. Examples of analytical texts can be found in professional and technical journals. Finally, some texts are written for the purpose of comparing phenomena. *Comparative* essays place two works side by side for the purposes of discussing similarities and differences. For instance, an essay comparing *Romeo and Juliet* with *West Side Story* is one example of a comparative piece.

These purposes also form the basis for the common structures presented within texts. Rarely do any expository texts focus on one purpose only. This observation is especially true for the texts written for children and adolescents. It is far more common for students to encounter texts that contain many purposes. Knowledge of these text structures is essential for building comprehension of expository texts, and we will discuss them in more detail later in this chapter.

The author's purpose for the creation of an expository text can provide valuable insight for the reader. In turn, the reader's purpose influences how he or she understands these texts. Students turn to expository texts for a variety of reasons, and these purposes are foundational to their discussions of them. At times, students use expository texts to understand the content being taught, as when they read textbooks. At other times, students use expository texts to build background knowledge about the content being taught. A student who is unfamiliar with the digestive system might turn to *Human Body* (Walker, 2009) for a visual tutorial of the organs and their processes. At other times, students may use a text for the purpose of researching a topic in depth. A student working on a project about the Donner Party disaster of 1846–47 for the upcoming social studies fair will look for texts that tell her about California migration, wagon trains, the geography of the Sierra Nevada mountain range, and cannibalism to augment the information about the event itself. Yet another purpose for using expository texts is for composing. A student who is writing a comparative essay for his U.S. history class might read to learn about World War II and the Vietnam War in order to develop a thesis on why the public's response to its returning soldiers was so different. Both the purpose of the text itself and the reader's purpose for reading it shape the discussions about it.

Expository texts cover a range of informational and persuasive purposes and represent a broad array of text types. In addition, readers approach these texts in highly individualized ways. Let's take a closer look at some of the reasons why expository text is so important and why it is more challenging than narrative text for many readers.

The Importance of Expository Text

It is truly exciting to see informational texts in the hands of the youngest readers. Visit any primary classroom today, and you will find leveled texts, big books, visual dictionaries, and concept books throughout. Many teachers organize part of their library around high-interest topics, featuring tubs of books devoted to spiders, dinosaurs, weather, and animals. This has not always been the case. In 2000, Duke reported on the dearth of exposure to informational texts for some first-graders. Her analysis of instructional time found that an average of only 3.6 minutes a day were devoted to the use of informational texts in all the classes studied, and in low-SES classrooms the average was an even more disturbing 1.9 minutes. She notes:

> Traditionally, the fourth-grade slump has been explained as resulting from the increase in demand for expository reading and writing that is thought to occur around fourth grade. Perhaps one reason this slump is reportedly more pronounced among low-SES students is that they have had

> less pre-fourth-grade school experience with informational text forms. Similarly, perhaps more low-SES students would develop a stronger interest in reading if their first, critical years of schooling offered a less narrow reading diet. (Duke, 2000, p. 221)

The notion of a reading diet has resonated with elementary educators, and publishers have responded positively to this need. Moss (2009) analyzed the two California basal readers for grades 1–6 and found that an average of 41.7 percent of the pages were devoted to expository readings. However, she also reported that argumentation and persuasion pieces were nonexistent in grades 1–5 and constituted only 7.95 percent of the informational texts in sixth grade. Moss further makes the point that students overall have little experience with this specific type of expository text and yet are expected to write persuasive pieces for state and national assessments in seventh grade (Moss, 2009). Given that it is widely accepted that informational reading and writing dominate the middle and high school years, it is in the interest of all educators that students be exposed to expository texts from their first years of school.

Tapping Into Students' Interests

Despite a persistent stereotypical notion that "girls like stories and boys like facts," studies of children's reading habits reveal that both genders like to read nonfiction. A study of the library checkout rates of 2,000 children ages seven to thirteen speaks to their reading preferences. By far, the most preferred subject was animals (33.9 percent), followed by science (15 percent). Sports and literature ranked third and fourth respectively for boys, while the reverse was true for girls (Sturm, 2003). This overall preference for nonfiction may be driven by the availability of informational texts for elementary-aged children, as well as better publishing techniques such as the use of color photographs and diagrams that fuel interest.

We use an interest survey with our students to find out about their interests and the ways they spend their time with print and digital media (see fig. 4.1). Rather than ask students about specific topics, we invite them to imagine two hours of uninterrupted time, with the only caveat being that they can't take a nap. We inquire about what they would do with that time (play something, create something, read something, and so on). We also ask them what kinds of things people come to them to ask about because they know a lot about the topic. Stanley told us that people ask him about dance moves (he is in a hip-hop dance crew), while Carmen said her friends know to ask her about *manga* and *anime*. Although none of these topics is strictly academic, the students' answers gave us insight about our resident experts in popular culture, which proved to be a boon throughout tenth-grade English. When it came time to teach about persuasion, we used opposing opinion editorials about reality television, rules for school dances, and violence in film as some of our topics.

1. Imagine that you have two hours of free time. No one is going to ask what you're doing or interrupt you to give you some other job to do. The only condition is that you can't take a nap. How do you spend that time? Please check your top three choices:

   ☐ Connect with your friends (in person, texting, social networking site)

   ☐ Make something new (build something with your hands, make music or art, compose on paper or digitally, enhance your virtual world presence)

      ☐ alone

      ☐ with other people

   ☐ View something (watch TV or a movie, check out a video-sharing website)

   ☐ Listen to something (music, podcast, audiobook)

   ☐ Play something (games, cards, video game)

      ☐ alone

      ☐ with other people

   ☐ Find something (information, how to do something new)

   ☐ Read something (book, magazine, online article, another person's blog)

2. What are your top six topics that you never seem to get tired of talking about?

   _____

   _____

   _____

   _____

   _____

   _____

3. Whenever someone has a question about _____, he or she comes to me for information about it.

   _____

   _____

   _____

   _____

   _____

Figure 4.1: Student interest survey.

Despite a demonstrated need for more student experience with expository texts, some teachers resist using them. Some elementary teachers fear that nonfiction will be of little interest to their students or that it may be too difficult to comprehend (Duke & Bennett-Armistead, 2003). Even among secondary teachers, it is not uncommon to see expository texts being used in limited ways, replaced instead by lecture. Some teachers say that they can cover the material through lecture more quickly than if students were to read about it (Armbruster et al., 1991; DiGisi & Willett, 1995). This may be true when the teacher covers only a narrow instructional range. In a classroom where the only sources of information are the teacher and the textbook, there's not much room for support. The problem with this model is that the act of reading and understanding is solitary and independent. Therefore, either students are lucky enough to "get it" or they miss it altogether. Since most teachers don't want to risk the latter possibility, they choose a lecture format for any class that struggles with informational text.

But what they have overlooked is the importance of discussion as a means for understanding expository writing. As noted in the previous chapter, read-alouds and shared reading can be effective means for building comprehension. Combine these methods with a broader array of conceptually rich texts and opportunities for discussion, and students will thrive (Ivey & Fisher, 2006).

Why Expository Texts Are Difficult

To be sure, expository texts as a rule are more difficult to comprehend than narrative ones. They require students to have experience with the form. In addition, elements such as concept load, specialized vocabulary, and an assumption of familiarity with certain concepts (background knowledge) make these texts more challenging.

Concept load refers to the amount of ideas packed into a passage. The density of these concepts can make it difficult for the reader to see all the relationships between these ideas. Consider this passage under the heading "Cell Structures" from a high school biology textbook:

> In a factory, there are separate areas set up for performing different tasks. Eukaryotic cells also have separate areas for tasks. Membrane-bound organelles make it possible for different chemical processes to take place at the same time in different parts of the cytoplasm. (Biggs et al., 2007, p. 193)

The paragraph is well written and has its audience in mind, especially in using the analogy of a factory to describe the workings of a cell. Even so, the concept load is pretty high. In these two sentences, the reader must understand what a factory is, deal with the technical vocabulary of *eukaryotic*, *organelles*, and *cytoplasm*, think about how a membrane works, and keep in mind that different chemical processes can happen simultaneously. The vocabulary gets some added support, as the diagrams are labeled and a sidebar explains that the prefix *cyte-* is Greek in origin and means *cell*. Background knowledge must be marshaled. Eukaryotic cells were first introduced and explained seven pages earlier, and cytoplasm first appeared two pages before this one. The textbook also includes a glossary and an index, but using them is at the discretion of the reader.

Talk about active reading! A tenth-grade student reading this passage has a lot to do to comprehend it. When does he study the diagrams, and which ones are most helpful? Does the student know that turning back to reread a section can be helpful? Does he know how and when to use the glossary and index? The word *membrane* doesn't appear in either the glossary or the index, although *plasma membrane* does. What can the student do if he needs help remembering how the membrane works and can't recall the inferred modifier *plasma*?

Text-based discussions can be useful in extracting the meaning from this dense text. After Eric, Khadijah, Jared, and Lexie read this passage in Mr. Bonine's biology class, they discussed it using reciprocal teaching (see chapter 4, page 79, for more on this method):

ERIC: So I'll summarize. There are lots of organelles in plant and animal cells, and they each have specialized jobs. You can look at the pictures on the other page to see all the parts of the cell.

LEXIE: And they talked about it like a factory. Here are some questions for you. What's a eukaryotic cell?

JARED: It's a cell that has a nucleus.

KHADIJAH: How'd you know that?

JARED: Because we talked about them on Tuesday, remember? And it's in the book (flips pages) here.

KHADIJAH: Ask us another question, Lexie.

LEXIE: Okay, what's the cytoplasm?

KHADIJAH: They didn't say it here, but they did on the last page. (Reads) "The environment inside the plasma membrane is a semifluid material called cytoplasm." Mr. Bonine said it was sort of like a jelly. It's all around the organelles.

JARED: I'm the predictor, so I'll make a prediction about what we'll read next. I can see that the next two headings are "The Nucleus" and "Ribosomes," so my prediction is we're going to read about each of the organelles in the diagram.

ERIC: (whistles) That's a lot, bro.

This discussion sets up the rest of the reading, which becomes more technical. The time the students spent on this opening paragraph allowed them to talk about terms and concepts, activate their background knowledge, and return to the text for supporting information. Because they were able to talk about what they understood, they collectively strengthened one another's comprehension and prepared for the more detailed content that will follow. Understanding the genre—in this case a science textbook—equipped the students with more cognitive resources to figure out how the information would be laid out. Students benefit from instruction on the kinds of genres they encounter in the classroom.

Genres of Expository Text

As we discussed earlier, genres refer to the content of the text. Knowing something about the genre gets you ready for the reading, and at times can prevent you from drawing incorrect conclusions. For example, when Nancy reads Frank Rich's column in the *New York Times*, she understands that it is an opinion piece and that opposing views exist. When Diane looks up a word in the *Oxford English Dictionary (OED)*, she expects a high level of accuracy and authority. When Doug reads the directions to change a tire on his bicycle, he knows he'll get a minimum of words and lots of diagrams.

Students need to know what to expect when approaching various kinds of expository texts. Further, when they are developing their own expository pieces, this knowledge gives them insight into what their audience will expect. Doug doesn't want the history of bicycles; he needs clear directions so that he can change the tire and be on his way. Diane expects to have some derivational meaning and word origin information when she looks up a word in the *OED*—that's why she chose it in the first place. And Nancy knows that she needs to seek out other opinion pieces to get a more nuanced view of a controversial topic.

Expository text genres run the gamut from narrative-style biographies and autobiographies to procedural manuals that feature concise text in sequential order. Other genres include concept books that focus on a topic, comparative essays, reference materials, life-cycle and nature books, experiment and activity books, and editorial cartoons and opinion pieces.

Biographies and Autobiographies

The story of a person's life, whether told in third person or first, makes for compelling reading. These books mirror many of the features found in other narrative texts, and they rely on a story structure. However, the reader should look for other textual elements that provide further authentication. Younger readers might find this information on the dust jacket, in the introduction, or as an end piece after the story. Biographies for older readers may include footnotes or an index of sources arranged by chapter. These textual features can be a focus of discussion. For example, Ms. Rothstein's second-graders used the back matter in *Nana Upstairs and Nana Downstairs* (dePaola, 2000) to discuss the picture book they had just read:

MS. ROTHSTEIN:	What clues did you use to decide whether this was fiction or nonfiction? When I look at it, it seems like fiction.
GEMMA:	It says, "This book is a true story."
JOHN:	But the pictures are all drawn, not like real pictures.
MS. ROTHSTEIN:	Do you mean photographs? That can be a clue about whether something is nonfiction.
BENJAMIN:	But he's an artist [referring to dePaola]. We read other stuff by him, and he always draws his pictures.
MS. ROTHSTEIN:	That's good to know some things about the author. Let's look back at this page about the book. What's another clue you can use?
CANDICE:	He has the whole names of his grandmas in the end. Their names are Honorah—how do you say that? Honorah O'Rourke Mock and Alice Mock Downey. Not Nana Upstairs and Nana Downstairs like in the rest of the book.
MS. ROTHSTEIN:	Why's that a clue for you, Candice?
CANDICE:	'Cause it sounds like real people, not pretend ones.

Concept Books

Books that focus on a single topic are another favorite of younger readers. Alphabet books for preschoolers often focus on one topic, be it insects, trucks, or food. The Eyewitness Books for Children series put out by DK Publishing has taken concept books to a new level with the inclusion of vivid photographs and illustrations on a bright white background. This series covers a broad range of topics, from life in a castle to robots.

Students in Mr. Balangue's seventh-grade social studies class were studying world religions and were focusing on the contributions of Islam to the cultural development of Europe, Asia, and Africa. A group of students read an excerpt from *Mosque* (Macaulay, 2003) and discussed the unique architecture of the buildings:

ZAIRA:	I had no idea it was a whole bunch of buildings.
JOSE:	Yeah, I thought it was just one, like when you go to a church.
REBECCA:	What was that word for it?
JOSE:	*Kulliye*. It says it's a complex, with like a school and a place for them to have meetings and stuff.
ZAIRA:	We're supposed to look for evidence in the book.
REBECCA:	There's the picture. It shows a whole bunch of buildings.
JOSE:	And there's a floor plan on page twelve.

> **ZAIRA:** And it says here (reading), "It consisted of an open prayer hall, a dome, a portico, a fountain, and a minaret."
>
> **JOSE:** (reading along) Keep going. It says, "Over time, the domed cube became the standard form for all the buildings of the kulliye, regardless of their function."
>
> **REBECCA:** What do they mean, "over time"? Like a long time?
>
> **JOSE:** I'm not sure. That's a good question. Let's keep reading.

Nature Books

Nature and life-cycle books have much in common with concept books in that they typically focus on a single topic. However, these books have their own organizational structures that make them unique. For example, they contain scientific information about an organism's habitat, range, diet, and structure. This information is often augmented with diagrams, maps, and timelines. Students reading nature books must often move back and forth between the words on the page and the visuals to fully understand the meaning of the information.

Fourth-grade students in Ms. Lincoln's science class were reading about lizards in the book *Reptiles and Amphibians* (Howell, 1993). Like many nature books, this one was segmented into self-contained sections that did not have to be read sequentially. The students stopped at a page describing the eyesight of lizards. The page contained quite a bit of information, and it was not clear what the students should read first. Although their approach was somewhat chaotic, they knew that the text wasn't strictly linear and that they had to work at finding the meaning across features:

> **BOBBY:** Look at that! That gecko's all pink and everything.
>
> **HEATH:** But that's not what this page is about. Look at the title, "The Better to See You."
>
> **BOBBY:** Like Little Red Riding Hood!
>
> **MITCHELL:** I'll read this top part to all of us.
>
> **BOBBY:** No, start here (pointing to the gecko).
>
> **MITCHELL:** We have to start at the top. Look, the letters are bigger here than on the rest of the page (reads the main part of the text).
>
> **HEATH:** So that's why chameleons change colors. They can see in color, so they can see each other.
>
> **BOBBY:** Now read the part about the gecko.
>
> **HEATH:** No, not yet. We're moving down the page. There's a cartoon of a boy lizard giving flowers to a girl lizard.
>
> **BOBBY:** That's not real. But the caption says they blush to attract a mate.

MITCHELL: And look at this picture! There's a chameleon looking at himself in a mirror, and he wants to fight himself. He's got all bright colors.

HEATH: So here's what we know. They can see in color, so they can change colors for fighting.

BOBBY: And for gettin' a girlfriend! Oooohhhh!

Reference Books and Search Engines

Reference books are organized so that readers can turn to the part they need, locate information, and then close the book up again. These books are not read cover to cover, but instead are intended to be dipped into (Fountas & Pinnell, 2001). The organizational structure is typically alphabetical or categorical to facilitate the location of information. However, if the reader doesn't know the organizational structure, the search for the needed information may be fruitless. Many teachers instruct their students on the use of alphabetical and categorical systems, especially with regard to using a thesaurus, a dictionary, or an encyclopedia.

Ninth-grade English teacher Ms. Roth knows that her students will be expected to write research papers in her class and in other content courses. She also knows that they increasingly obtain their information electronically. However, despite a general demeanor that suggests her students know everything about technology, they are not especially adept at using search engines efficiently to yield useful information. Therefore, Ms. Roth makes sure that they know how to use advanced search engine tools so that they can locate information quickly, dipping in and out of the Internet in much they same way they do with printed reference materials.

Ms. Roth models the techniques by using a computer and whiteboard hooked to the school's Internet service. She introduces advanced search operators: words that preface search terms and are followed by a colon and then the desired information. (There's no space after the colon.) She begins by typing in "earthquake" and generates 38,600,000 hits—far too many to weed through. Then she refines her searches by using the following operators:

- **Inurl.** Refines the search to web addresses that feature the key terms. Therefore, *inurl:earthquake* yields 3,160,000 webpages with the term *earthquake* in the url address.

- **Site.** Limits information to the domain name. Ms. Randall demonstrates that typing *site:usgs.gov earthquake* narrows the search to the 336,000 websites within the domain of the United States Geological Survey.

- **Intitle.** Further restricts the search to identifying terms in indexed titles. A search of *intitle:earthquake+usgs* locates 217,000 indexed titles and documents that contain the words *earthquake* and *USGS*.

- **Link.** Narrows a search to links to a particular website. For example, the entry *link:www.usgs.gov* shows the 5,590 websites that have linked to this url address.

Experiment and Activity Books

Books that require active participation remain popular with many students because they capitalize on the students' sense of inquiry. Nancy recalls buying this type of book for her own children to keep them busy during summer vacations. However, these books are used inside classrooms as well.

Mr. Rodriguez requires students to use activities from his collection of such books as part of their participation in his ninth-grade earth science class. Each week, one group of students completes the activity or experiment and presents it to the class. Several students selected an activity from *Earthsearch: A Kid's Geography Museum in a Book* (Cassidy, 1994) on contour topography. Following the directions in the book, they created a contour map of the topography of their hands and then told the class about it:

OMAR: We did this experiment right here (holds up book) about making a contour map on your hand. See? (The students all display the back of their hands to the class.)

MR. RODRIGUEZ: Why did you pick that one?

CHEYENNE: We've been talking about maps of geological formations, and this one caught our eye.

LUSI: We mapped the Knuckle Range of the Four Finger Mountains (giggles). What? That's what it said in the book!

MR. RODRIGUEZ: That's okay. It is funny. How did you do it?

OMAR: Well, the directions said to make a fist on the table and draw circles of the same distance all the way around the peaks . . .

CHEYENNE: That's the knuckles . . .

OMAR: . . . and then mark blue for the rivers between the fingers.

LUSI: When you lay your hand out flat, the circles aren't all the same distance apart. Just like on a contour map.

MR. RODRIGUEZ: And what do those variations in circle width symbolize?

OMAR: The elevation.

MR. RODRIGUEZ: Excellent! And good luck explaining why you have all those lines on your hands when you get home tonight.

CHEYENNE: I'll just tell them it's all in the name of science.

How-to Books and Procedural Manuals

Like experiment and activity books, procedural manuals are organized sequentially. Unlike experiment books, their purpose is not to facilitate discovery of a new concept, but rather to provide directions on how to complete a task. Procedural manuals rarely provide any background information or state a larger concept. The measure of whether readers have understood a text of this type is their successful completion of the task. These texts can be challenging for a reader who does not have much background information, because they generally assume that the reader possesses certain knowledge.

For example, recipes are a common form of text in Ms. Pereira's family and consumer sciences class. Students come to the class with a wide range of knowledge and experiences. Some have never boiled water, while others routinely prepare dinner for their families. Therefore, Ms. Pereira has students follow recipes in groups, since the directions are often sparse, and the genre assumes a functional amount of background knowledge. A recipe for blueberry pancakes was a challenge for some members of one group. The students assembled the necessary ingredients but had not read through the recipe in its entirety. Therefore, they initially ignored the "large mixing bowl" clue that suggested they would need another bowl. When they read that they needed a separate bowl in which to mix the milk and egg, they had to stop to retrieve it. Ms. Pereira saw this and joined the group. She encouraged the students to read the recipe all the way through—not just the ingredients—so that they would know what utensils were needed as well. When they did so, they questioned what the term *fold* meant in the recipe. This gave Ms. Pereira an opportunity to reteach the specialized vocabulary the students would need to successfully make pancakes.

Editorial Cartoons and Opinion Pieces

Opinion pieces often employ persuasive techniques and argumentation (see chapter 2). Students benefit from knowing where they are likely to encounter opinion pieces. Traditionally, newspapers and magazines have explicitly labeled this type of writing as "opinion." However, an increasing number of opinion pieces appear, unlabeled, in Internet blogs. For this reason, opinion pieces can easily be disguised as objective pieces. Advertisements can also masquerade as informational pieces. It is necessary to teach students about the uses of persuasive techniques and argumentation so that they can recognize the difference between opinion and fact.

Editorial cartoons are a unique form for expressing opinions, and they can provide a window on the sentiments of a time and people. History teachers often use editorial cartoons from the past two centuries to illuminate controversies and opinions of the time. Mr. Morris, a high school economics teacher, uses political cartoons for this purpose. During a unit on wage differences between men and women, Mr. Morris gave his students a Doug Marlette cartoon about this inequity, as well as a cartoon analysis worksheet designed by the education staff of the U.S. National Archives and Records Administration (2011). Using the worksheet to guide their discussion, the students analyzed the Marlette cartoon, which had two panels. The first panel showed a man behind an office desk with a framed dollar bill behind him. The second panel showed a young woman, also at a desk, with a framed "First 59 cents" on the wall behind her. In small groups, the students listed the objects, people, and words they saw in the cartoon. The discussion then shifted to symbols and emotions:

MR. MORRIS: Let's talk about symbols. What are you seeing?

DAISY: The man is an older guy with a suit on, and he looks like a businessman.

HECTOR: Kinda fat and happy.

YUSEF: But the woman's got a lower desk and a lower chair.

AJA: Yeah, the guy's got a big chair. It's high in the back. Over his head.

DAISY: And she's typing.

HECTOR: The old guy has his hands folded.

MR. MORRIS: What about their emotions? Look at their faces.

AJA: He's got a big grin, and she has no mouth at all.

YUSEF: She's mad.

MR. MORRIS: What's she mad about?

DAISY: She has less money.

MR. MORRIS: How do you know?

DAISY: She's got that "first 59 cents" in her picture, and the old guy's got his first dollar.

MR. MORRIS: So what do you know about this time in history? It's probably the 1970s.

HECTOR: That's part of what the Equal Rights Amendment was supposed to do. Equal pay for equal work.

MR. MORRIS: But are they doing equal work? Look again.

AJA: No, it looks like she's the secretary, and he's the boss.

MR. MORRIS: You're right. The artist is commenting on more than just equal pay. He's also commenting on equal opportunities. So here's your next discussion point. What special-interest groups might have agreed or disagreed with this political cartoon?

Structures of Expository Texts

Like narrative texts, expository or informational texts have an internal structure. While narrative texts are structured around story grammar (setting, plot, characters, conflict, and so on, as described in chapter 3), informational texts typically use one of five basic structures:

1. Description or list

2. Cause and effect

3. Problem and solution

4. Compare and contrast

5. Sequence

Description or List

This type of text provides rich descriptions of events or places and often includes a listing of attributes. Typically, when an author uses this structure, there is a main idea for the paragraph with lots of details within the paragraph. The following excerpt fits this text structure:

> The ocean is its own world, with mountains, valleys, volcanoes, and a wealth of animals from tiny to huge. Here are some of the things we know about the ocean:
>
> - The ocean formed about 4½ billion years ago.
> - The ocean is 96.5% WATER and 3.5% DISSOLVED SALT.
> - Ocean water stores HEAT. It keeps the world from getting too cold.
> - The ocean holds almost all LIVING MATTER on earth—97%.
> - Most of the OXYGEN we breathe comes from plants in the ocean. (Daniels, 1999, p. 6, emphasis in original)

Cause and Effect

This type of text presents a relationship between specific events and the impact of those events. As the text becomes increasingly complex, the effects are often the subsequent cause, which then leads to another effect. The following excerpt fits this text structure:

> By 1940, Germany ruled most of Europe. Great Britain was Hitler's next target. He ordered deadly submarines, called U-boats, to sink any supply ships headed to Britain. U-boats were so successful that starvation and defeat were a real possibility for Britain. (Nicholson, 2005, p. 21)

Problem and Solution

This type of text presents readers with a problem and then the solution that addressed it. Sometimes, the solution becomes the next problem, and sometimes the solution is successful. Readers typically find this type of text satisfying because the author presents a problem, often one that the reader cares about, and then shows how it was solved. The following excerpt fits this text structure:

> Many people are fearful of ancestors and restless spirits. To prevent a person's spirit from haunting them, Zulu men in South Africa walk backward while carrying the body to its grave. They believe this will confuse the spirit of the dead so it cannot find its way back to haunt the living. Many East Asian cultures believe that tending the graves of their ancestors by weeding or sweeping and making frequent offerings will keep the dead

content so they will not come back as ghosts or vampires to make trouble. (Sloan, 2002, p. 8)

Compare and Contrast

This type of text provides information about the similarities and differences between things. Readers of this type of text get information about two or more things at the same time. The following excerpt fits this text structure:

> Some delegates admired Samuel Adams as a political idealist, a visionary. Others saw him as a crank, a revolutionary fanatic, a rabble-rouser who "eats little, drinks little, sleeps little, thinks much, and is most decisive . . ." in the pursuit of his objectives. A rumpled man with a kindly face, magnetic blues eyes, and an iron will, he cared nothing about wealth, social position, or appearance. His clothes were so shabby that friends in Boston bought him a new outfit so that he would not embarrass Massachusetts when he went to Congress. Those who knew him were astounded when he showed up in Philadelphia wearing a handsome wine red suit and carrying a gold-handled cane. (Freedman, 2000, pp. 27–28)

Sequence

This type of text presents information in some type of order. In using this structure, the author provides the reader with a schema for remembering the information, whether it be chronological or procedural. The following excerpt fits this text structure:

> This is the Street of a town in pain that cries for the Drug known as cocaine, made from the Plants that people can't eat, raised by Farmers who work in the heat and fear the Soldiers who guard the Man who lives in the House that crack built. (Taylor, 1992, p. 13)

Within the sequence structure—as within the other four major text structures—there are a number of subtypes. How-to texts, such as the technical manuals we discussed earlier that describe how to build or fix something, are sequence texts. In addition, sequence texts can be chronological, such as texts that relate a series of historical events in the order in which they occurred. Another type of sequence text explains a process, such as cell division.

Signal Words

Signal words are often useful in helping readers identify the type of text they are reading. Table 4.1 includes a list of common signal words organized by text structure. Importantly, as texts become increasingly complex, they offer fewer and fewer signal words. As a case in point, take a moment to reread the problem and solution example. While it is clear that the author is discussing the ways different cultures address the problem of fear, the common signal words used in this type of text are absent.

The goal is not to have students read a text and simply identify the structure that the author used, but rather to predict how the text will work. When readers attend to the text structure, they are more likely to remember what they read. Noticing the internal text structure also helps students when they need to return to the text to find additional information. As Dymock (2005) and Moss (2004) note, students must be taught to use the text structures, especially since informational texts are not commonly used in many elementary school classrooms (Duke, 2000).

Table 4.1: Text Structures and Signal Words

Text Structure	Definition	Signal Words
Compare/ Contrast	A text that describes the similarities and differences between two or more things, places, events, ideas, and so on.	although, as well as, as opposed to, both, but, by contrast, compared with, different from, either . . . or, even though, however, in common, in comparison, instead of, like, on the other hand, otherwise, similar to, similarly, still, unlike, whereas, yet
Problem/ Solution	A text that identifies an issue and how the issue is solved. Often the solution becomes another problem.	because, consequently, despite, dilemma is, if . . . then, problem is, puzzle is solved, question/answer, resolved, result, so that, thus
Cause/Effect	A text that explains how or why something happened.	accordingly, as a result of, because, begins with, consequently, effects of, for this reason, if . . . then, in order to, is caused by, leads/led to, may be due to, so that, steps involved, thereby, therefore, thus, when . . . then
Chronological/ Sequence/ Temporal	A text that presents information in order of time, sequence, or as a process.	additionally, after, afterward, another, as soon as, before, during, finally, first, following, immediately, initially, last, later, meanwhile, next, not long after, now, on (date), preceding, second, soon, then, third, today, tomorrow, until, when, yesterday
Descriptive	A text that provides details that could be a list or outline.	above, across, along, appears to be, as in, behind, below, beside, between, down, for example, for instance, in back of, in addition, in front of, in particular, looks like, near, on top of, onto, outside, over, specifically, such as, to the right/left, under

Source: Fisher, Frey, & Lapp (2008a), p. 89.

The goal is not to have students read a text and simply identify the structure that the author used, but rather to predict how the text will work. When readers attend to the text structure, they are more likely to remember what they read. Noticing the internal text structure also helps students when they need to return to the text to find additional information. As Dymock (2005) and Moss (2004) note, students must be taught to use the text structures, especially since informational texts are not commonly used in many elementary school classrooms (Duke, 2000).

When students have been taught to recognize and use text structures, they often return to the text and provide evidence from it to bolster their arguments. For example, in a discussion about the beginnings of the French Revolution, students regularly used their knowledge of text structure to make their points. As part of their group conversation about the text, Mohammed said, "Remember that there were rich people and really poor people? That contrast really helped get the revolution started." Hanan replied, "Where did you find that? I was thinking about the problems the people had trying to live. The solution, at least I think it will be the solution, is a civil war. When people aren't happy with their government, there's a revolt. Like what happened in my country, but not as big as this one."

Text Features

In addition to the internal structure common to informational texts, most texts of this type use features designed to assist the reader in making sense of the information. We will provide a list of common text features, knowing that all texts do not include all of the features. Having said that, when students return to the text, these features can help them locate information and use that information in figuring out what they understand and where they still have questions. We've grouped the text features into four categories that should provide a schema for their relative functions and usefulness.

Print Features

Print features help the reader locate information through organization. Unlike some text features, print features have existed in texts for decades, if not centuries. As readers, we can use the table of contents, index, glossary, preface, introduction, and appendix to find information quickly.

For example, while completing a lab in their sixth-grade science class, a group of students got confused about the difference between potential and kinetic energy. Knowing that the textbook provided definitions and examples of these terms, Kaytlin turned to the index and found *energy*, then located the specific type of energy she wanted to review, saying, "It's here on page 127. That's where I found the examples." In this case, returning to the text was necessary for clarification, and the print features that Kaytlin knew how to use facilitated her retrieval of the information that the group needed to proceed.

Illustrations

Visual information can be added to a text to enhance the meaning of the words. During the past century, more and more visual information has been added to texts. These visuals typically include photographs and drawings that represent the main ideas of the text. Importantly, the illustrations do not simply summarize the text but often expand the meaning of the text so that students arrive at a greater understanding of the text when they attend to the visuals.

In terms of how our brain attends to and remembers information, illustrations consistently trump text or oral presentations. This phenomenon is so well documented that cognitive scientists have a name for it: *picture superiority effect* (Stenberg, 2006). In essence, when students are taught to attend to the visual information presented in a text, they remember more content. For example, when a group of sixth-grade students used graphic novels to review their social studies content, their discussions went deeper, and they recalled more of what they had read. As part of their review of early humans, the students read *The First Civilization: Fire and Error* (Fisher & Frey, 2008a), a sample of page of which appears in figure 4.2 (page 98). In their conversation, the students returned to the text and illustrations to discuss early humans. At one point, Serena commented, "There were a lot of discoveries, for not having much. I mean, really, they lived in caves and didn't have much clothes, but they figured out fire and how to be safe from the animals that wanted to eat them."

Organizational Aids

Like print features, organizational aids help readers find information. The difference is that organizational aids are within the text, and print features surround the text. As readers, we use bold print, italics, bulleted lists, headings and titles, captions, labels, and sidebar information when we initially read and when we return to the text to find information. Unfortunately, many struggling readers do not know how to use these organizational aids and thus have a difficult time knowing "which pieces of information encountered in expository text are most important and which can be filed away as unnecessary" (Bluestein, 2010, p. 597).

When students do use organizational aids, they can both determine importance within the text and return to the text to provide evidence for their claims. Most textbooks include very intentional organizational aids that students can use to understand the content. For example, in our adopted social studies book, the headings are in red, and each section includes a main idea statement. These features are quite helpful, and students use them regularly in their note-taking and discussions.

Trade books and popular press publications also include organizational aids. For example, students in a tenth-grade U.S. history class had heard the book *Six Days in October: The Stock Market Crash of 1929* (Blumenthal, 2002) read aloud to them. While creating a collaborative poster on which each member of the group used a different color marker, students returned to the book that was read to them, as well as to a

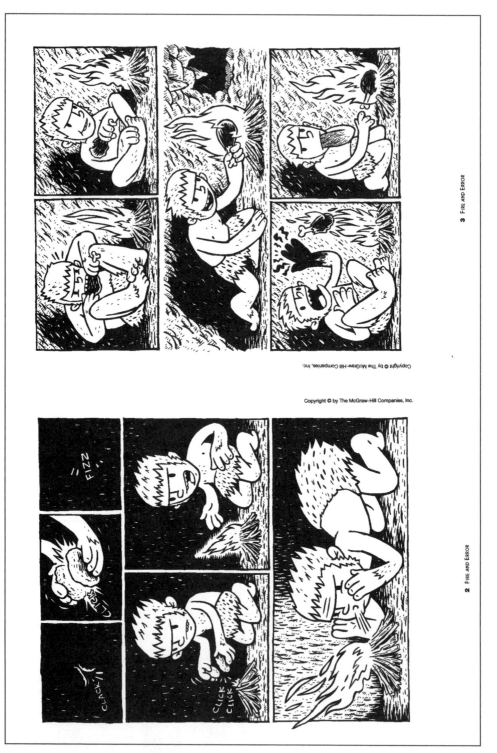

Source: Fisher & Frey (2008a). Used with permission.

Figure 4.2: Sample page of a graphic novel.

number of other informational sources, to verify information and ideas. At one point, Crystal's group disagreed about the reasons people put their money into the stock market. David made the case that people thought it was safe. Ahmed countered that banks were safer. Crystal, returning to the text, showed her group members a 1929 political cartoon from *Forbes* magazine and focused on the caption, which noted that ordinary people thought that they could get rich quickly in the stock market. David made a connection with another time in U.S. history: "It's like when the Gold Rush happened. Everybody's always thinking that there is a quick way to get rich." Ahmed added, "And he says right here, 'more people than had ever before gambled their savings in such a risky and unpredictable place as the stock market'" (Blumenthal, 2002, p. 4). Looking at the page again, Crystal commented, "Oh, now I get all of those little letters and numbers on the bottom of every page. They're the prices, and look, they are getting lower."

Graphic Aids

The final category of text features is the largest and perhaps the most significant. In many texts, information is represented in specific ways that combine visual and textual features. Graphic aids, such as diagrams, graphs, charts, figures, maps, tables, and timelines, provide readers with important information that is often not specifically stated within the text itself. Importantly, students frequently use these graphic aids when they need to understand something deeply. When students use graphic aids to understand the reading, they are pushed deeper into the content and can return to the aids when they need to be reminded, have questions, or need evidence.

For example, when the students in Ms. Martinez's third-grade class were planning their trip to the zoo, they read from a map provided by the zoo, which contained information about each of the exhibits and the animals within the exhibit. Each student had a copy of the map and met with two other students to plan the trip. Each three-student group had a chaperone, but that person did not plan or influence their trip through the zoo. As evidence of these third-graders' use of graphic aids, consider the following exchange that took place within one group:

> **HEATHER:** So where should we start? How about with the new elephant area? It's right here (pointing to her map).
>
> **JACOB:** I love the elephants! And I wanna see the polar bears. They are right here (pointing on Heather's map).
>
> **AMBER:** Those are far apart. And look, the elephants are way to the back. Could we start with animals that are closer?
>
> **JACOB:** Yeah, we can. But we're gonna see the polar bears, right?
>
> **HEATHER:** Yeah. Where do you want to start? Remember, the purpose is to observe five different animals and how they adapt.

AMBER: What about the flamingos? Those big pink birds who stand on one leg? They are at the front of the zoo.

JACOB: Everybody will do that. Would you go to the panda bears? They are right here (pointing to his map).

As students become accustomed to using graphic aids, they apply this knowledge to a wide variety of reading situations. Our high school students do this all of the time as they negotiate primary-source documents and unlock the meaning of these texts.

Specialized Vocabulary

We've chosen to focus on vocabulary in this chapter on expository text, not because words are irrelevant in narrative texts, but because the words used in informational texts are often more specialized and technical in nature. In narrative texts, authors frequently use interesting and complex words once in their writing. These are called *singletons* and can make reading more difficult. Narrative texts introduce readers to words such as *trustworthy*, *dramatic*, and *melancholy* (DiCamillo, 2000). Readers might be able to figure out the meaning of a singleton from the context and perhaps even add the word to their known vocabulary. Sometimes, knowing the word is not required to get the gist of the reading. Other times, the teacher can provide a definition or an example, and understanding is maintained. That's not to say that the words used in narrative texts are not worthy of being taught, but rather that when interesting words occur once in a reading, the risk is that they'll be forgotten. If the words are worthy of being taught, students need repeated exposure to and practice using the words (for example, Hiebert, 2005; Scott, Skobel, & Wells, 2008).

Deciding which words to teach has been a source of significant concern for teachers (Graves, 2006). In general, there are three types of words (Beck, McKeown, & Kucan, 2002; Vacca & Vacca, 2007). Tier 1, or general, words are the everyday words readers use, such as *pesky*, *vacation*, and *rowdy*. Tier 1 also includes sight words such as *when*, *does*, and *you*, which are often not easily decoded and must be memorized. Tier 2, or specialized, words are words that change meaning in different contexts or contents. Consider the list of words in table 4.2. These words have common definitions but also have specific meanings in science, which really serves to confuse students. And finally, Tier 3, or technical, words are those terms that have a specific meaning and are typically used in one content area (for example, *meiosis*, *guillotine*, and *rhombus*).

While understanding the different types of words can help teachers narrow down a list of words to teach, this system does not provide enough guidance for selecting words. Consider the following text from the National Assessment of Educational Progress, administered to fourth-graders in 2007, and think about which words would have been worthy of instruction:

> I must get help, said Rosa to herself. But how? I don't know anyone. Mama told me not to speak to strangers. Besides, I don't know how to ask in English.
>
> Rosa had an idea. She rushed back to the street, walked to the traffic light, then raced around the corner and back to the school yard. (Springer, 2007)

Table 4.2: Specialized Science Vocabulary

Word	Common Definition	Scientific Definition
tissue	Thin paper Facial tissue	A group of the same type of cells that performs a specific function within an organism
rod	Any long, cylindrical object A boy's name	A photoreceptor in the eye that distinguishes the shapes of objects
vessel	A container for holding something A ship	A tube through which a body fluid travels
culture	The social customs of a group of people	The process of growing living tissue in a laboratory
petrified	Made rigid with fear	Turned into stone by the replacement of tissue with minerals

We have developed criteria for selecting words worthy of being taught. These criteria apply to both narrative and expository texts. We've organized them into six categories and provided questions to consider for each category (Fisher & Frey, 2008c, p. 26).

1. Representation
   - Is the word representative of a family of words that students should know?
   - Is the concept represented by the word critical to understanding the text?
   - Is the word a label for an idea that students need to know?
   - Does the word represent an idea that is essential for understanding another concept?
2. Repeatability
   - Is the word used again in this text? If so, does the word occur often enough to be redundant?
   - Will the word be used again during the school year?
3. Transportability
   - Will the word be used in group discussions?
   - Will the word be used in writing tasks?
   - Will the word be used in other content or subject areas?
4. Contextual analysis
   - Can students use context clues to determine the correct or intended meaning of the word without instruction?
5. Structural analysis
   - Can students use structural analysis to determine the correct or intended meaning of the word without instruction?
6. Cognitive load
   - Have I identified too many words for students to successfully integrate?

With these criteria in mind, it's easy to see why the specialized and technical words commonly found in expository texts are often included in lists of words worthy of being taught. The specialized and technical words commonly found in informational texts are also the ones that are necessary for text-based discussions. It's hard to talk about earthquakes if you don't understand the term *fault* or the phrase *fault line*. Without these terms, the discussion is at risk of focusing on personal experiences rather than a combination of personal experiences and scientific information.

Our point here is not to focus on how to teach vocabulary, as there are many excellent resources available on the topic. Rather, our point is to focus on the role that words play in reading and discussing texts. As you'll see in the section on instructional routines later in this chapter, understanding words and being able to use them appropriately is one of the indicators that students comprehend the text. When students own the words, meaning that they can use them correctly and independently, the connections they make with the text are enhanced.

Resources on Vocabulary Instruction

Block, C. C., & Mangieri, J. N. (2006). The vocabulary-enriched classroom: Practices for improving the reading performance of all students in grades 3 and up. *New York: Scholastic.*

Frey, N., & Fisher, D. (2009). Learning words inside and out: Vocabulary instruction that boosts achievement in all subject areas. *Portsmouth, NH: Heinemann.*

Graves, M. F. (2009). Teaching individual words: One size does not fit all. *New York: Teachers College Press.*

Yopp, H. K., Yopp, R. H., & Bishop, A. (2009). Vocabulary instruction for academic success. *Huntington Beach, CA: Shell Education.*

Consider the conversation a group of fourth-grade students had about a text they were reading called "Astronauts in Training" (Telicki, 2007). The words targeted for instruction included *endless, realistic, universe, astronaut, sensible, protested,* and *paralyzed*. In this excerpt from their conversation, the students use several of the words:

> **BETHANY:** It's not very realistic, saying that they're going to Mars.
>
> **ADAM:** Yes it is. They are realistic because people have gone to space before.
>
> **LISA:** I agree with Adam. But, like it says, they have to train. It's not really realistic for just anyone to go to space. They have to be strong enough and get ready.
>
> **BETHANY:** But how will the astronaut that is paralyzed get strong enough? That's what I was meaning about realistic.

ADAM: I don't know. Maybe it's because of gravity out in the universe and he won't be as paralyzed.

LISA: Remember, Ms. Robeck said that *paralyzed* can mean powerless or helpless, like the example of the person paralyzed by fear.

BETHANY: But I don't think that's what they mean here because it says that he was paralyzed since he was a child, so I think it means really paralyzed.

ADAM: Like the kind when you can't move your legs or something. That's what happened to my uncle. He got paralyzed because he crashed his motorcycle.

BETHANY: Exactly. So would it be realistic for your uncle to go into space? It's not sensible.

Each student had taken notes individually as he or she read the text and then took additional notes during the discussion. After the group discussion, each student summarized the conversation and their notes. Without attention to these words, the group conversation and task would not have been as productive and would likely have veered away from the text and the understandings that can be gained from reading and discussing expository information.

Useful Instructional Routines for Discussing Expository Texts

Because we are unable to be with every student every moment throughout the period or the school day, we rely on classroom routines that we and our students have created and agreed upon. Organizational routines give students and teachers clear expectations of what should occur throughout the day, how the time will be divided and managed, and what will happen during these various time periods. When precise and well-shared organizational routines are in place, students quickly realize what is acceptable behavior for working alone, with peers, with the teacher, and with the teacher and peers. They know which task to work on, the participants, the material sources, the due dates, the grading procedures, and where to look for support when they need it. Once the classroom routines are taught, consistency using them ensures that students have uninterrupted opportunities for learning and teachers have uninterrupted time for instruction (Colvin & Lazar, 1995). Students know how to operate independently and collaboratively in the learning setting.

In addition to organizational routines, teachers can use instructional routines that support students as they independently read and converse about text. Teachers need to introduce students to these routines, which are often referred to as *instructional strategies*. Instructional strategies or routines designed to promote text-based discussion are those that empower students to take ownership of their reading and learning, to make personal connections, and to appreciate that one text can have multiple interpretations (Spiegel, 1998). As students participate in text-based inquiry and discussion, they begin to realize that reading is a valid activity that is vital in their lives, and that it is through the reading of content-based, topically related sources and also collaborative conversations about the information they are reading that they are able to expand their bases of knowledge and subsequently negotiate personal meaning (Knickerbocker & Rycik, 2002).

As described earlier in this chapter, readers often view expository texts as being more complex because of the topical knowledge being conveyed through very dense ideas, unfamiliar technical vocabulary, complex text structures, and unfamiliar text features. The teacher plays a major role in teaching students instructional routines or practices that support their learning of content information. Just as in teaching students any new information, the teacher must always provide a gradual release of the responsibility for learning. Through modeling and guiding students as they learn content information and routines, the teacher's role changes from being the source of, or provider of, information to being a support to students as they deepen their content knowledge and independence. We share the following instructional routines as examples of practice that will help students become actively engaged in text-based collaborative discussion and learning.

Thinking Aloud With Expository Texts

We introduced the idea of read-alouds and shared readings in chapter 3. This same procedure can be used with expository or informational texts. For example, while reading aloud from *If A Bus Could Talk: The Story of Rosa Parks* (Ringgold, 1999), the teacher stopped to think aloud about what the author had told her readers about Rosa Parks's educational experiences:

> *The author tells me that Rosa Parks was in class with fifty to sixty other students. That's a lot of people in one room. Look at our classroom. I see only thirty students. So that would be like double us, or all of us and all of Mr. Booth's students in the same classroom with just one teacher. I can visualize that because the author tells me some specific information. I'm thinking that wasn't the best way to get your education, but it could work. But then the author says that the school only went up to sixth grade, but the school for white students went up to twelfth grade. Okay, so now I'm upset. I want to know why the black students had to stop their education at sixth grade. I'm wondering if that was because society expected them to go to work earlier, or something. It's hard to imagine, now, that students only got to attend school up until sixth grade. There is so*

much to learn! I wonder how Rosa Parks knew so much. I better read on and find out more about her education.

The teacher continues, reading aloud and pausing to share her thinking, always returning to the text to provide answers or ask additional questions. Sometimes, the teacher disagrees with the text or questions the assumptions in the text. For example, when the author talks about Parks's husband being "light skinned," she questions the assumptions about skin tone. She also invites students to periodically talk with a partner about the text so that they can make connections with the reading and remember to return to the text for additional information. For example, at the beginning of the reading, when the bus has no driver, the students are invited to talk with a partner about what's happening in the story. Several students hypothesize that the bus has been hijacked, others propose that the story is fake, and still others think that the character Marcie is dreaming. The teacher reminds them to return to the text to find out more.

A Grade 10 Biology Think-Aloud

A biology teacher we know uses a very similar process, but he projects the text using a document camera. His shared readings highlight scientific thinking as well as comprehension strategies. He is very conscious to model returning to the text to check his assumptions and recollections against what the author has said. He starts his shared reading with a comment to his students, usually some variation of "I read to find things out, and sometimes I find out things I didn't know, and other times I find conflicting information. I have to be very careful and pay attention to what the author says so I don't make mistakes. That doesn't mean that I agree with, or believe, everything that I read, but that I'm paying attention to the author and what I think."

One day, he was reading from *Fish* (Schleichert, 1997), comparing and contrasting freshwater and saltwater fish. At one point in his shared reading, he paused and said,

> *So there are more types of fish that live in saltwater than freshwater. I've never really thought about the numbers, but this author is saying that there are about twenty thousand kinds of fish. Of those, only about eight thousand live in freshwater. I really thought it would have been the opposite, because it seems more difficult to survive in the harsh conditions imposed by the salt in the ocean and sea. I'd like to know more about how fish survive in the saltwater. I'll keep reading and see what I can find out (reads more of the text). And there it is: the author tells me that cold-water fish that live in saltwater have a protein in their blood that is an antifreeze, like the fluid we put in our cars so that they don't freeze up in the*

winter. I'm going to take notes on this aspect of the saltwater fish, as I think it will come in handy when I need to summarize the differences between the types of fish.

Text Impressions

This instructional routine helps students become familiar with content language and passage information by reading actual words and phrases that the teacher has taken from the passage they are about to read. As they read the list, the students make predictions about the information that is contained in the target passage. Text impressions help students think about the text when pre-reading, during reading, and after reading. Teachers can use this routine with a whole group, in smaller partner teams or groups, or with individual students. Similar to story impressions, a routine that was designed by McGinley and Denner (1987) to help students make predictions and then comparisons about setting, character names or descriptions, plot, and resolution, text impressions focus on a non-narrative passage. Whether they will be reading a story or an expository passage, students become familiar with the language and concepts they will be meeting.

To begin creating a text impression, the teacher makes a list of ten to fifteen key words or phrases that support the meaning of the text. He or she arranges the words vertically to indicate the order the words appear in the text and also the order in which they should be read. The students are invited to read the words orally with the teacher and to work together as a whole class or in pairs to make predictions about the meaning of the passage they will read. Either as a whole class or in pairs, the students then use the words to write a paragraph that conveys their prediction of the passage contents. The students share their paragraphs and then read the target passage. After reading and discussing the target passage, they compare it with the prediction paragraphs they wrote and then edit the prediction paragraphs to match the target text.

When we introduced our students to text impressions, they shared that the routine really helps them when they read unfamiliar text because, as Omar said, "It gives us kind of a mental outline." Our students now request that we create text impressions for them each time they read any new text independently or collaboratively.

A Grade 4 Geography Text Impression

Let's see how a fourth-grade teacher used a text impression to prepare her students, who were studying volcanoes, to read a passage about Mount St. Helens. Her list of targeted words and phrases from the passage appears in figure 4.3.

Mount St. Helens

Mountain

Washington

Volcano

Floating pieces of land

Earth's surface

Moving, slipping, sliding

Overlapping plates

Bottom

Heated

Melts

Pushed down

Center of earth

Liquid rock and gases

Pushed up

Earth's surface

Great pressures

Figure 4.3: Fourth-grade text impression word list.

To begin, the teacher explained to the students that they would be reading a text about Mount St. Helens, which is a volcano in the state of Washington, which is located in the Pacific Northwest region of America. Next, she displayed the vertical list on the document camera and explained that she had created it from the actual text the students would be reading. She invited the students to read the list orally with her. After they had read these words as a whole class, she told them that they would next work in pairs to write a paragraph about Mount St. Helens. She cautioned them to use the targeted words in their paragraph in the exact same order as she had listed them. When the students finished, they shared their work as a whole class. The following paragraph comes from a fourth-grade English learner and her partner:

> **Mount St. Helens** is a **mountain** that is in **Washington**. It is a **volcano**. There are **floating plates of land** near Washington in the **earth's surface**. Sometimes there is **moving, slipping** and **sliding**. Some of the **overlapping plates** go to the **bottom** of the **heated mountain** and **melt**. They can get **pushed down** to the **center of the earth** and then turn to **liquid rock and gases**. Next, they get **pushed up** out of the **earth's surface** and cause a lot of **great pressures** with people.

You can see that these two students have a lot of knowledge about volcanoes, but some of their understanding about *liquid rock and gases* and *great pressures* needs to be clarified by reading the actual text. After the two students completed their paragraph using the words from the list, they and the other partner teams compared their writings to the online article about volcanoes that was the target text. As the students read, they were able to return to their prediction texts to check their accuracy and to make changes as needed. Like our students, these fourth-graders were highly motivated to read as they used text impressions as an organizing frame.

Reciprocal Teaching

Reciprocal teaching is another instructional routine that supports readers in socially constructing meaning making through text-based discussion. Before asking the students to independently apply reciprocal teaching, the teacher must describe and model the routine and also discuss how it aids comprehension. Reciprocal teaching occurs as a dialogue among four students, who assume the roles of summarizer, question generator, clarifier, and predictor as they attempt to gain meaning from a text they are reading. Palincsar and Brown (1984) conducted a series of studies on the effectiveness of reciprocal teaching as an instructional routine. Their findings suggest that this approach not only supports comprehension but also results in greater student engagement with text and fewer off-task behaviors.

To implement reciprocal teaching successfully, the teacher must thoroughly model each role and then offer support to students as they start working in their teams and attempt to assume the role he or she has modeled. To be sure that students understand all roles, the teacher might want to have them switch roles before asking them to use reciprocal teaching without his or her help. By switching roles, students better understand what each one involves and can, therefore, support their peers who later assume the various roles.

To begin using reciprocal teaching, we model each role in a fishbowl style; then we invite all members of the class to become teams of four and to work together practicing each role. Students need a lot of practice before reciprocal teaching becomes a natural routine. However, once students are able to employ it effectively, they always state how well it supports their developing comprehension of the target information. Becoming more confident in their abilities to analyze text supports their expanding knowledge bases and interests in reading.

Grade 3 Science Reciprocal Teaching

A third-grade teacher decided to use reciprocal teaching to help her students understand the non-narrative text they were reading in a *Weekly Reader* news magazine. Over the course of several days, she modeled each of the four roles until she felt the students were familiar with what the task entailed and their responsibility to the group. Then she had the students gather in their four-member groups and assigned each student a role: predictor, question generator, clarifier, and summarizer. As you read the following dialogue from one group, notice how the students returned to the text often to support their thinking:

LUZ (Predictor): So before we read this article on Earth Day, I predict that it'll tell us ways to help take care of the earth. Look at these headings. They give us clues about what's happened to the earth, how we can help, and our future.

BRAD (Question Generator): I wonder when Earth Day is, anyway. I also wonder if our earth has gotten any cleaner because of all the recycling we do.

SAMUEL (Clarifier): Okay, let's read the first few paragraphs and see if Luz was right with her predictions.

(STUDENTS READ)

JESSE (Summarizer): Before I summarize, do you have any questions?

BRAD (Question Generator): Yes, can somebody explain global warming? I'm still confused.

SAMUEL (Clarifier): Maybe this photo and caption will help?

JESSE (Summarizer): This paragraph right here explains it, too. Let's reread, and then I'll summarize.

In this example, each of the students knew to return to the text in support of what he or she was thinking. Luz, the predictor, used the headings and key words to help her predict what the article would be about. Brad knew that the bolded words (Earth Day and global warming) were important, and so he asked for clarification. Samuel, as the clarifier, knew that returning to the text involved looking not only at the words but also at the pictures and other graphics. Jesse, the summarizer, illustrated that she knew enough about this non-narrative structure to guide her group to look for explanations and definitions of the bolded vocabulary words.

These children became adept at using reciprocal teaching to guide their reading and discussion because their teacher had thoroughly modeled each role before she had asked them to work as an independent group. She had also given them practice with each role so that they were able to support their peers when the group met on its own.

Graphic Organizers With Relational Words

Nearly every book about comprehension instruction written since the 1950s has suggested using an organizational chart (Durrell, 1956; Earle, 1969; Herber, 1970; Vacca & Vacca, 2007; Wood, Lapp, Flood, & Taylor, 2008). Commonly referred to as *study guides*, *semantic maps*, or *reading guides*, graphic organizers provide a visual representation of information that is being read. The information within a graphic organizer is succinctly categorized in a manner that supports learning and remembering. Many variations of graphic organizers exist because they are specifically designed to fit the organizational structure of each text type. We (Lapp, Fisher, & Johnson, 2010) have found that

> students who create their own graphics improve their understanding of what they read, remember the salient features of texts, and are more confident in their retellings. We also found that by adding relational words to their maps their retells are fuller, more accurate, and they exhibit even greater confidence in their retellings, even when probed. Importantly, this finding crosses both narrative stories and recounts of nonfiction or content-based texts. We believe that the combination of relational words and student-created graphics provides familiarity and the language cues students need to support their remembering, connecting, and sharing information. (p. 424)

A Grade 5 Science Graphic Organizer

A group of five fifth-grade students gather in the library with their textbook and a clipboard. Their task is to read and discuss information about the digestive system. This group of students knows that making a graphic organizer is helpful for understanding non-narrative text. The following dialogue shows how they create a graphic organizer to help them negotiate the meaning of a text they are reading about the digestive system:

IAN: Gosh, our bodies are complicated, and there's many facts in this section.

ADAM: There sure are. Let's see maybe if we start at mouths, where the best part happens.

JOHANNA: That's right. Since digestion happens in a particular order, let's make a graphic organizer that shows how this happens.

MAX: Good idea. Let's not use the one we used yesterday. The semantic web won't work well for this. We need one that shows a sequence.

ADAM: Okay, I'll draw it. I'm going to start at the top and write "teeth."

SHANISHA: Yeah, and then draw a picture next to the word because pictures help me remember. Let's add "tears and crushes food" 'cause that's what the book says.

MAX: Okay. Next comes the tongue. That's important in digestion.

JOHANNA: It is, but I think we should add in "saliva" before "tongue."

MAX: Why?

JOHANNA: Well, look here (pointing to the text). It says saliva helps to soften the food in the mouth so that it is easier to swallow. You gotta have the saliva before the tongue can do its job.

MAX: Okay. That makes sense. How are you going to draw saliva?

SHANISHA: Just like this (shows her picture).

MAX: Cool! It looks like melted ice cream.

ADAM: Let's add some words between "teeth" and "saliva" to help us understand this better.

IAN: How about "afterward"? That will remind us that AFTER the teeth do their job, the saliva does its job. Then we can write "together with" that leads to the word "tongue." All of these little words help me to remember.

JOHANNA: Yes, and they remind me how everything fits together.

MAX: Okay, I'll write "together" because we know that saliva and the tongue have to work together.

SHANISHA: Don't forget to make a little sketch next to the tongue, too!

By introducing students to routines such as graphic organizers, we are ensuring their independence as readers who can comprehend what they are reading as they organize the information, creating visuals and connecting words that remind them of important details.

Note-Making

Being able to take notes is a very practical and functional study skill. Our early forms of note-taking begin when we jot down details from a phone message or information conveyed in any form that we hope to remember. There are two types of notes (Fisher & Frey, 2011): those that we take while someone is talking or while we're watching a video (which is known as *note-taking*) and those that we take while we're reading (which is known as *note-making*). The main difference between the two is whether you can return to the source and check your notes again. When listening to a speaker, it's hard to rewind the person the next day to check the accuracy of your notes. It's much easier to return to a text to verify information. With technology, the lines between note-taking and note-making are blurring. We have students who record class discussions (with permission) so that they can return to the conversation later to check their notes. YouTube and other storage systems allow for easier retrieval of videos. For our purposes here, we'll focus on note-making, as we are interested in teaching students to return to the text as part of their discussions and writing.

When we read nonfiction texts, we are seeking information. Making well-constructed notes allows us to organize and retrieve this information. There are many formats for note-taking and note-making, including common graphic organizers. Whichever approach you select to share with your students, you should first model it during a reading, writing, and retelling activity. Once you have introduced your students to a variety of note-making routines and formats, it's important to invite them to select the format that works best for them.

Grade 9 Note-Making

As a group of three ninth-grade students gather to discuss *The Jim Crow Laws and Racism in American History* (Fremon, 2000), they use note-making as a strategy to comprehend what they are reading. These students have been taught various ways of making notes from text (Cornell note-making, graphic organizers, and Foldables™). The following dialogue gives us a glimpse into their conversation as they read, write about, and discuss the Jim Crow laws—specifically the *Plessy v. Ferguson* case in 1896—all the while returning to the text for clarification and to check the accuracy of their thinking. When the students mention "our paper," they are referring to the Cornell note-making page (Pauk, 1974) they are using to record the information they agree on. This tool contains three areas: a narrow column on the left, a major column on the right, and a space at the bottom to write a summary (see fig. 4.4, page 114).

DEVON: It seems like this case was one of the most important during this time period.

OSHARAY: Sure was. Look here, almost this entire chapter is about *Plessy v. Ferguson*.

SYRAH: Let's start making some headings on our paper about this.

OSHARAY: I'm going to stick with the five Ws: who, what, where, when, why.

SYRAH: Good idea. So let's make those headings on the left-hand side of our paper.

DEVON: We'll fill in the information about each on the right-hand side.

SYRAH: Yes. So let's see. We should probably start by reading what the case was about.

(STUDENTS READ)

DEVON: So you mean this guy Plessy got thrown in jail because he was black?

SYRAH: Yeah, one-eighth black. His skin was very light.

OSHARAY: So I'm going to write next to my Who column, "Plessy was black man; got thrown in jail."

DEVON: I would add that he had light skin . . .

SYRAH: Or that he was one-eighth black because that's significant.

OSHARAY: Why?

DEVON: Well, it says right here that they chose Plessy in the first place because he *could* buy a train ticket because he was light skinned, and then he announced onboard that he had African American ancestors. Everyone wanted to see what would happen. It goes back to the separate but equal chapter we read yesterday.

SYRAH: Yeah, and it says it happened 1896, so let's add that to the When column.

DEVON: Okay, so now we know that Plessy, who was a light-skinned black because he was only one-eighth black, got thrown into jail for announcing he was black in 1896.

OSHARAY: Why did he announce it?

SYRAH: Let's keep reading, and when we find out, we'll put it in the Why column.

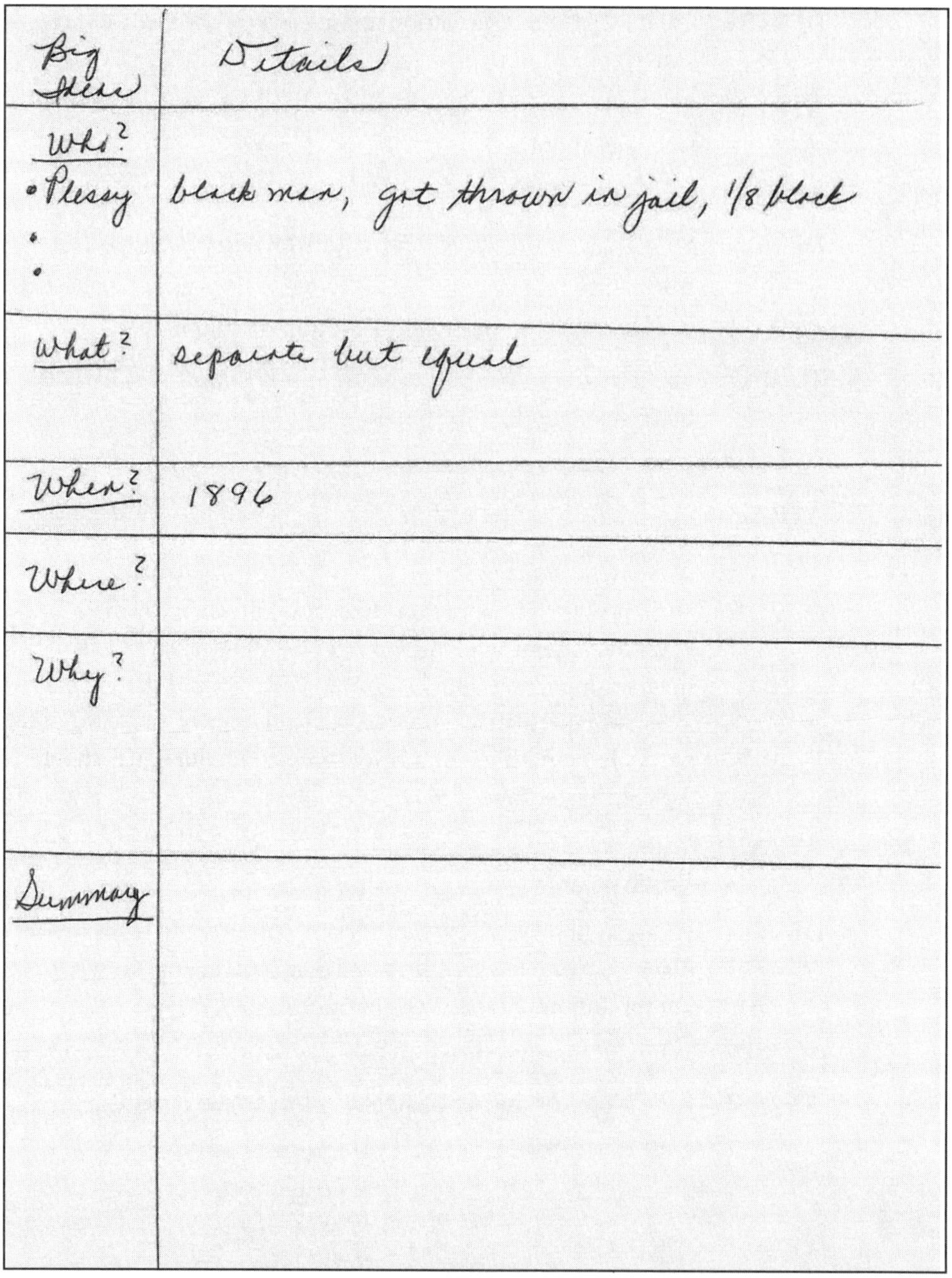

Big Idea	Details
Who? • Plessy • •	black man, got thrown in jail, 1/8 black
What?	separate but equal
When?	1896
Where?	
Why?	
Summary	

Figure 4.4: The students' Cornell note-making page.

While these students were using the Cornell format, other students were using a Foldable to record the same information (fig. 4.5, page 115). Foldables are interactive graphic organizers that provide structure and organization for students and also serve as excellent study guides or resources for further projects.

Figure 4.5: The students' Foldable note-making page.

Regardless of the form that students use, note-making and note-taking help them to internalize the information they are gaining from the text and from their text-based collaborative conversations. Learning to take and make notes is a must routine, especially as students are seeking information from many text sources and text types.

Summarizing

Summarizing is a complex strategy that requires significant amounts of practice. Proficient readers identify main ideas and supporting details and then organize and synthesize this information into smaller units. They pause to think about what they are reading, and in doing so, they continually add new information to the base of comprehended information. An ongoing strategy, summarizing occurs as we attempt to get the big ideas while reading and also when engaging in conversation. In 1989, Pressley, Johnson, Symons, McGoldrick, and Kurita examined comprehension research to determine which strategies most significantly affected one's comprehension. Summarizing is the one they listed as first.

As teachers, we need to help students summarize in ways that will support their synthesizing key chunks of information instead of attempting to hold on to every detail. Paris, Wasik, and Turner (1991) observe that less-proficient readers never summarize and proficient readers wait until the end to do so. By then, they have too much information to remember, especially if they are reading content information. The researchers suggest that summarizing needs to occur continuously while reading and listening instead of at the conclusion. Examining one's summary allows for metacognitive monitoring of a personal interpretation of the passage or conversation.

By inviting young children to offer retellings, teachers are able to highlight the importance of retelling as a measure of understanding. Our modeling should illustrate how to delete erroneous information and how to use one's own language, rather than the language of the text, to combine and condense information into bigger chunks. Such modeling identifies ownership of what is being read. It's also important for teachers to model the practice of checking a retelling against the information in the text in order to be sure that as readers we have not misrepresented the information the author has shared. Through our modeling, students become aware of the task as well as the process of summarizing.

Grade 7 Summarizing

Students often have a difficult time summarizing text because they are not able to make sense of long passages, confusing vocabulary words, and difficult sentence structure. By using GIST (generating interactions between schemata and text) as a summarizing technique, students can chunk the text to make it meaningful to them. The GIST strategy (Cunningham, 1982) helps students read expository text and get the main idea. After reading three to five paragraphs of a text, they must capture the "gist" of what they are reading in a sentence containing exactly twenty words. Then they read the next three to five paragraphs and add another twenty-word sentence to the summary paragraph they are creating. They repeat this process until they reach the end of the text. This routine forces readers to continually evaluate their sentences and to squeeze out all extraneous information. To model GIST, teachers may, in advance, read a passage of about twenty paragraphs and create one-line summaries that they can compile into a total summary. As the students read and create their own summaries, they can check their GIST statements against the teacher's model summary.

In the following example, a seventh-grade teacher thinks aloud about how she is summarizing the information she is learning while reading an article about immigration laws. Notice how she returns to the text often to check for the accuracy of her summaries.

I can see that this article on immigration is very long. I see that the author already chunked it into five paragraphs. After I read each, I will write a summarizing sentence of not more than twenty words. This will give me a summary paragraph that is five sentences long. Okay. I'm going to read this first paragraph aloud. Listen and see how I think about the important parts of this paragraph. [Teacher reads.] I see that they are giving a bit of history about immigration in the United States. It also talks about several different states and how every state has their own unique laws. I don't need to list all those states in my summarizing statement, but I will write the gist of what the author is trying to say. How about:

There are many states and each state has a different immigration law.

Okay, now let me return to that paragraph to see if that's right. [Teacher looks back at the text.] Well now, let's see. It doesn't say that all the laws are different from one another. It says that they may be different. This means that some might be the same. I better change my summarizing statement to reflect what the author is really saying. I'll change my sentence that summarizes this first paragraph to:

Many states in our country may have different laws about immigration.

By summarizing for her students in this way, the teacher models how to summarize text and how important it is to capture relevant, accurate information by returning often to the original source.

Figure 4.6 (page 118) is a chart that students can use to summarize a five-paragraph article. If the article has more than five paragraphs, the teacher needs to model for students how to read three to five paragraphs before writing a GIST statement. Often, the subheadings in an expository passage help readers to know when to stop and summarize.

Conclusion

As the examples in this chapter have shown, when students read text and engage in text-based discussions, meaning making is an individual task that is supported through routines and interactions that enable the construction of information. Practicing these routines is how students will meet the expectations of the Common Core State Standards. One of the anchor standards is that students must be able to "cite specific textual evidence . . . to support conclusions drawn from the text" (Common Core State Standards Initiative, 2010, p. 35).

Paragraph #	One-Sentence "Gist"
1	
2	
3	
4	
5	

Summary (all five "gist" sentences combined):

_____

_____

_____

Figure 4.6: GIST summarizing guide.

The routines we've shared provide frames that support accountable talk about a text. Going well beyond opinion, the students in our examples used insights from the target texts to make predictions. They then read and also returned to the text to find support for their thinking, to clarify information about which they were unsure, and to check facts. As they engaged in these routines, they became very metacognitively aware as they realized how to support their own comprehension.

To help students become independent meaning makers, teachers must model metacognitive processes early, presenting them as strategies that contribute to comprehension. When modeling a routine, teachers should talk about how their comprehension is growing and note that they are aware of this because they are monitoring or paying attention to their increasing understanding of the text. With practice, students will then effortlessly use these routines to support their text-based learning across the many text structures of expository text.

CHAPTER 5
Analyzing and Discussing New-Media Texts

AFTER DIANE AND SEVERAL of her students took a field trip to see *The Twilight Saga: Eclipse*, they had a conversation about some early cultures' fascination with drinking human blood. People in these cultures believed that drinking the blood of another human enhanced their vitality or "lifeblood." Although the idea of cannibalism in any form seemed horrific to these students, when presented as a behavioral possibility for Stephenie Meyer's 104-year-old Edward Cullen, it evoked a more sympathetic response:

LADONNA: I know it's a form of cannibalism, and many prehistoric groups in the South Pacific thought this was okay, but really, Edward would never do anything so awful as suck blood if he could help it—especially never Bella's.

KIKI: I know, huh. He loves her.

ANGEL: He would even fight Jacob for her.

ANDY: He's still a vampire. You forget this cuz you be thinkin' he's handsome.

LADONNA: Maybe, cuz I thought the same thing when I saw *Dracula*.

KIKI: I think you like movie stars, not vampires.

LADONNA: No, I still thought it when I read the book. He was so smart and polite. I could hardly picture him doing anything so nasty. I think the same about Jacob. I couldn't choose between him and Edward. One on each of my arms! Too hot!

ANGEL: Let's see: a vampire or a werewolf. If they even exist.

MALIK: It's fun to think about. Maybe we know some.

DIANE: Could still be possible, if you really believe in vampires. I love the fun of it, but I really do think it's pretty fictional—but who knows for sure. I really liked *Eclipse* better than *New Moon* because I felt that it gave me a better view of each character and also more information about vampires. The whole idea has always intrigued me. I'm going to read the short story "The Master of Rampling Gate" by Anne Rice [1984] on my new iPad to see if her vampire is similar to any of the Cullens. [One family of vampires in the Twilight series by Stephenie Meyer has the surname Cullen.] I'll let you know if there are photos included of the Master and if he seems as likable as Edward; can't say I found Dracula as appealing.

MALIK: I'm still reading *Dracula*. He is so intense, and I like how he transfers his Dracula powers to others. I'd like to be able to climb like he can.

KIKI: Yeah, I finished *Dracula*, but I liked how he could change weather. If I didn't feel like going to school, I'd just make a bad storm. Now I want to read the new book about Bree Tanner. She is such a little vampire.

ANDY: (whispers in an eerie voice) But still a vampire who could suck your blood and turn you into a newbie. [A newbie is a newborn vampire who is created from a human who is killed by a vampire. It is exceptionally strong because it still has the strength from what remains of its human blood.] Let me take a group picture to put on Facebook just in case one of you isn't at our next meeting.

Before separating, the students and Diane agreed to continue their study of "vampires in film and literature" and to set a meeting time to chat in two weeks. Diane reminded them to come ready to support their responses with connections from the text and from their life experiences.

The students in this episode belonged to a literary book club in Diane's class, one of many book clubs at the high school where we teach. These clubs all follow similar procedures: After the students and their teachers select themes, which must relate to the Common Core English standards, they identify multiple theme-compatible texts that accommodate a range of difficulty levels. Teachers, of course, slip in a classic or two. Each book is nominated in any format that the nominator believes will attract enough interest to have it selected as a book club read. Several students have presented their nominations as book trailers since we modeled this option for them with iMovie, which is the movie editor on a Mac. We did this because we are always looking for ways to ensure that students comprehend what they are reading, especially as they read increasingly more Internet-based sources and ebooks.

Expanding Notions of Reading, Writing, and Sharing Texts

While reading "The Master of Rampling Gate" on her iPad, Diane became involved with all of the additional links that offered information about events such as the Black Death (bubonic plague), descriptions of the Mayfair neighborhood in London, an interview with Anne Rice, and definitions of many, many terms. While she was delighted with all of the ancillary knowledge she was gaining, Diane realized that she had almost lost the primary thread of the novella, which she found herself having to reread several times. As Diane, Nancy, and Doug discussed this experience, we realized that as students read online, they are having very similar experiences to Diane's. She noted that she felt as if she had gained a breadth rather than a depth of knowledge. Like Diane, our students often leave the electronic text in pursuit of related information but fail to return to the original text and comprehend the author's perspective.

Moreover, as indicated by Andy's intention to document the vampire study group's day with a Facebook photo, most users of Web 2.0 now, in addition to reading information sources online, create content that they share online. Realizing this expanse of possibilities, many classroom teachers ponder how to develop their students' abilities to read, write, and communicate via opportunities with digital texts and new literacies.

To begin to develop an answer to this question, we must first begin with a broadened perspective that reading as meaning making now occurs as students interact with sources beyond a printed text. In addition to having the book as an information source, students now act as consumers and producers of information through their constant connections with the web, text messages, cell phones, and social networks such as Facebook and MySpace. Their multimediating practices (Gainer & Lapp, 2010; Lankshear & Knobel, 2003)—combining visuals, sound, and print—allow them to acquire, remix, and share information using the modes they feel are best matched to the content.

Breathe a sigh of relief if you are wondering if students are comprehending and composing as well when developing hypermedia as when reading and composing traditional texts, because Hobbs (2004; 2007) and Hobbs and Frost (2003) found that the comprehension and writing performances of students involved in media-literacy activities surpassed those of their peers who were involved in traditional literacy activities. These findings come as no surprise to those of us who are digital immigrants (Prensky, 2001). After attempting to construct a hypermedia message, we better understand the layered thinking of our students, the digital natives who not only read, but are also able to, at some level, "understand the power of images and sounds, to recognize and use that power, to manipulate and transform digital media, to distribute them pervasively, and to easily adapt them to new forms" (New Media Consortium, 2005, p. 4).

In the remainder of this chapter, we explore possibilities for cultivating and supporting these developing strengths in a school environment, and we consider how we can differentiate literacy instruction to accommodate the existing differences among students who have and have not had daily opportunities to read and develop new-media texts.

What Are New-Media Texts?

Digital texts may include visuals, sounds, movement, graphics, language, animation, and spatial dimensions. Because such possibilities did not exist before the global Internet, texts with these components are often referred to as *new-media texts*. Wysocki (2004) describes them well:

> We should call "new-media texts" those that have been made by composers who are aware of the range of materialities of texts and who then highlight the materiality: such composers design texts that help reader/consumers/viewers stay alert to how any text—like its composers and readers—doesn't function independently of how it is made and in what contexts. (p. 15)

As she suggests, students no longer view themselves as only being able to receive information shared by their teachers or the sources they have identified. Their behaviors which illustrate their abilities to create and share information reflect their understanding of both the expanding capabilities of technology and the communication purposes of the user. This combination has resulted in a need to reconsider what being literate means (Lapp, Flood, & Fisher, 1999; Rassool, 1999) and then to use this information to study ways to support students as they master proficiency in all areas of literacy. We believe the results of such study will strengthen dialogue across contexts and between students and their teachers.

Because of their vast connection opportunities, students—even those in the elementary grades (Zawilinski, 2009)—are communicating with and receiving information from continually expanding global audiences who have opened the context of their classrooms beyond four walls. In fact, findings from a study conducted by Blackboard (2010) and Project Tomorrow indicated that approximately one of every four high school students, or 27 percent, had completed at least one of their classes online. Although this was an increase of 13 percent over the previous year, many students reported that they were unable to take online courses because of the cost factor and/or because the classes they wanted were not available.

The Blackboard (2010) study also surveyed student teachers and found that only 4 percent of them reported that their methods courses had prepared them to teach any segment of their future courses online. Articles appearing in education journals describe current teachers as having even less formal bases of Internet knowledge but possessing an awareness of their students' insatiable interests in these multilayered experiences, which they seize as a potential bridge to school. Many teachers even communicate content with students through web-based assignments and converse via texting and social networks. We offer this comparison as a way of applauding educators who are attending to their students' online interests and practices in order to better understand how their instruction can advance their students' learning, especially the adaptation, modification, and expansion of their literacy processing to new-media contexts.

Understanding Comprehension

Several cognitive processes must be operative if comprehension is to occur in a way that supports a reader's being able to critically interpret and respond to what he or she reads. The reader must be capable of utilizing his or her language, must possess existing knowledge of the topic of the text, must be able to decode and assign meaning to words with a level of fluency, and must be able to use reading strategies as needed.

Assuming that readers speak the same language they are being taught to read, it is fairly obvious that what must then occur is the development of their understanding that the sounds of the language are represented by letters that, when blended together, make words. It is also fairly obvious that the more words readers know, the better able they will be to understand what they are hearing or reading. This link was well demonstrated by fourth-graders who received five months of vocabulary instruction in a study conducted by Beck, Perfetti, and McKeown (1982). On all subsequent tests of comprehension, the students who experienced vocabulary instruction outperformed the students who had not received it.

Vocabulary is also learned through wide reading, as was demonstrated by Morrow, Pressley, Smith, and Smith (1997). Having background knowledge that is related to the topic being read also supports comprehension. Although almost thirty years ago Anderson and Pearson (1984) shared that one's comprehension is dependent on knowledge of the topic, McKoon and Ratcliff (1992) later found that readers do not always draw on their prior knowledge to support their comprehension. However, through intentional instruction, readers can be supported in learning how to use all of these processes to strengthen their comprehension.

Proficient Reading

Using all of their bases of knowledge in combination, proficient readers assign their knowledge of letters and language to words, which they read with enough fluency to support making sense of the text. In other words, decoding, while certainly important, is not enough. As Samuels (2007) notes, simply teaching students to "bark at words" (or speed read) is not enough to significantly improve their understanding. Readers need to free up working memory to focus on meaning, which is why fluency is such an important process in comprehension. Proficient readers also make use of a repertoire of strategies such as previewing, predicting, questioning, inferring, visualizing, synthesizing, and summarizing (Pressley & Afflerbach, 1995). Because we discussed each of these strategies in more detail in chapter 1, we only restate them here to further illustrate their importance and to reiterate that, while they are identified as single strategies, they do not occur one at a time, but instead are bundled during comprehension processing (Pressley & El-Dinary, 1997).

As we have illustrated through the examples shared throughout this text, as readers are taught to interrogate themselves and the text before, during, and after reading, they learn to

> connect prior and new information, synthesize large chunks of information to support remembering, reread and monitor their speed to ensure their understanding, reflect and revise their knowledge based on new insights gained, continually evaluate the truth or worth of the information, summarize to support remembering the major thesis, and then apply and expand this knowledge to create new knowledge (Lapp & Fisher, 2009a, p. 3)

While it is essential for students to gain proficiency with each of these processes, we also want to stress the importance of motivation as a factor in the construction of knowledge and in the learning process.

Motivation

Motivation, which is a prerequisite and corequisite for learning (Bohn, Roehrig, & Pressley, 2004) arouses students' desire to participate in a task and sustains them throughout the process until their knowledge construction is complete. By establishing a classroom environment that honors students' voices and allows for choice, teachers enhance students' engagement, participation, and learning (Guthrie & Wigfield, 2000). To illustrate motivation as a factor in learning, we will discuss readers' engagement and comprehension as they explore new-media texts.

Understanding Web 2.0 Comprehension

To develop an understanding of how to support students' comprehension as they read new-media sources, it's first necessary to have a picture of what this type of reading entails. Yes, if students had their way, it would be one hand on the computer, one on the cell phone, one earplug in, and one ear left free for the teacher. As Richardson (2006) notes, "We are no longer limited to being independent readers or consumers of information . . . we can now collaborate in the creation of large storehouses of information" (p. 2).

We also no longer read in only one text or in a linear fashion (Spiro, 2006) but instead draw information from multiple forms of text that "afford not just a new way to make meaning, but a different kind of meaning" (Hull & Nelson, 2005, p. 225). Readers' ability to make sense of this assemblage of images across multiple formats certainly calls for a broadening of our understanding (Flood & Lapp, 1995) of how students comprehend and of how we can support their comprehension during hypertext reading activities.

To this end, Davidson and Goldberg (2009) help us realize that proficient Web 2.0 learners are not passive, nor are they simply consumers. Instead, they are constructors of information who, while reading multitudes of sources, make judgments regarding the validity and connectedness of sources, sites, and information.

Before continuing this discussion, we thought you might enjoy a side trip that will help you more fully understand how it feels to use hypertexts, which are linked electronically to information sources outside of the one being read. We invite you to spend some time visiting these sites: www.eastgate.com/ReadingRoom.html and www.digitalfiction.co.uk. Each hyperlink on these sites is designed to take the reader to information that can elaborate the base of understanding through related vocabulary definitions, audio, and graphics. While reading these texts, notice how you are not reading linearly, as you would a print-based text. Also, notice how you feel when interrupting your reading to go on new explorations. Even more significantly, pay attention to see if, by visiting hyperlinks, your comprehension of the content is enhanced or diminished.

We hope your experiencing of these hypertexts helped to illustrate Spivey's (1997) description of the complexity of readers' behavior while reading hypertext: "shap[ing] their meanings with organizational patterns, mak[ing] selections on the basis of some criteria of relevance, and generat[ing] inferences that integrate material that might seem inconsistent or even contradictory" (p. 191). Coiro and Dobler (2007) use the term *forward-inferencing* to describe the reader's ability to draw inferences from multiple sources and instantly evaluate the relevance of the connected information. They believe this process is one of the major differences between online and offline comprehension. After analyzing the think-alouds and interviews of skilled sixth-grade readers during and after they engaged in hypertext readings about tigers, Coiro and Dobler (2007) conclude:

> The skilled readers in our study engaged in a multi-layered inferential reading process that occurred across the three-dimensional spaces of Internet text . . . combining traditionally conceived inferential reasoning strategies with a new understanding that the relevant information may be "hidden" beneath several layers of links on a website as opposed to one visible layer of information in a printed book. . . . Internet reading seems to demand more attempts to infer, predict, and evaluate reading choice . . . to require readers to orient themselves in a new and dynamic three-dimensional space . . . to figure out how to get back to where they were. (p. 234)

> It became clear that each reader had constructed not only his or her internal understanding of a certain text, but had also constructed a unique external representation of the Internet texts most applicable to their needs. (p. 241)

In addition to being very able to predict, infer, and evaluate and synthesize information, these readers also had highly developed metacognitive abilities that allowed them to consciously monitor their meaning making.

Although the readers Coiro and Dobler (2007) and Dobson (2007b) described were exploring factual information sources, Dobson (2007a) gained similar insights regarding comprehension processing when she questioned adolescents about their readings of hypertext novels. As an aside, it's interesting to note that those students who were often annoyed by the hypermedia linking possibilities when they were reading, eagerly used hyperlinks in their writing. However, as they read, they were very aware of what they needed to do in order to make sense across links. This mindfulness on the part of the reader was also noted in studies conducted by Tierney and his colleagues (Galindo, Tierney, & Stowell, 1989; Tierney, 2009; Tierney et al., 1997), who found that "students appeared to approach hypertext with more questions, and more interest but with more concern over form (e.g., the layering of materials with links and interface with video) than the regular print-based projects" (Tierney, 2009, p. 226).

Reading in these virtual, digital environments has been nicknamed *three-dimensional reading* because it allows the reader to go deeper into texts. Print-based texts are two-dimensional, in that they are read from left to right and top to bottom. Three-dimensional texts are also read left to right and top to bottom, but the reader can also click on any hyperlink and go deeper. Importantly, this capability does not imply that the reader learns more or has a deeper understanding of the text. In fact, it may be that the reader loses the thread and never returns to the original text. In some situations, and for some purposes, this is not only acceptable but desirable. If a reader is looking for specific information, 3-D reading will most likely result in the discovery of that information. However, if comprehension of a topic is the goal, 3-D reading may interfere with understanding.

Implementing Web 2.0 Classroom Instruction

The following example takes us inside a middle-grade classroom where Ms. Johnson is using a gradual release of responsibility model as her instructional frame. The gradual release of responsibility frame that shifts the responsibility from the teacher doing all of the cognitive work to the students involves four components: focus lessons (purpose setting and modeling), guided instruction, productive group work, and independent learning. Ms. Johnson is remixing her knowledge of this model, her knowledge of a commonly taught curriculum topic, and inquiry-driven instructional practice that models for and supports her students' comprehension when reading new-media texts.

First, Ms. Johnson introduces the purpose for the lesson: she wants her students to understand and use persuasive oral monologues as a way to share information. The topic she has chosen to help her accomplish this purpose is one that many middle and high school students find interesting: the rise of child labor and the need for child labor laws in America during the Industrial Revolution.

Modeling: Introducing Topical Knowledge and Language

To begin a lesson on child labor laws, a teacher might share *Kids at Work: Lewis Hine and the Crusade Against Child Labor*, by Russell Freedman (1994), with photographs by Lewis Hine. This book uses text and photographs to examine child labor in U.S. fields and factories in the early 20th century.

In order to build background knowledge with students, Ms. Johnson shows the photographs on the document camera while thinking aloud about the images. As she does so, she explains that authors, speakers, and photographers share their voices through their oral language, written text, and selected graphics. In addition to looking at and reading these sources of information, she has her laptop connected to the projector so that she can model how to search online about a topic. Modeling this real-world researching is valuable because she often tells her students that one source never gives us all the information we might want or need. By using articles online, especially ones with hyperlinks, she can further model how her own wonderings take her on a journey, from text to cyberspace, in order to answer her queries. Table 5.1 (page 128) shows how Ms. Johnson thinks out loud about multiple texts.

Ms. Johnson, through thinking aloud, has begun to influence students' understanding that children who were placed in the workforce at a young age certainly had the opportunity to be exploited. She has also modeled the power of reading images as a way to develop domain knowledge. Ms. Johnson has also characterized the author's presentation of images and words as a monologue. She added a different twist to the usual sense of "monologue" by suggesting that an author/speaker can share a one-person perspective through a medium other than words.

Guided Instruction: Assessing, Supporting, and Guiding Students' Growing Understandings

After modeling how to think and talk about the photographs, Ms. Johnson invites the students to take a turn doing so. This activity will allow her to assess their growing understanding of the topic, language, and format. She shows a photograph from the book and guides her students to think about what they see and to posit what the children in the photos must be thinking. She asks her students to talk in pairs or in small groups about what the children in the photos might be saying to themselves, to one another, to their employers, and to other people who visited their work site. As Ms. Johnson mingles among the students and listens, she is able to assess whether

Table 5.1: Teacher Modeling With Visuals

What the Photograph or Teacher Shows	What the Teacher Says
On the cover of the book, there is a young child standing on a large machine, perhaps a cotton gin.	"On the cover, I see a small child on a very large machine. I know this book is about child labor laws. Could this child REALLY be working on this machine? It seems so complicated and dangerous for a young child. I wonder what that child is thinking."
A group of young boys is standing shoulder to shoulder looking unhappy. The caption reads: "Breaker boys at a Pennsylvania coal mine."	"I wonder what all of these young boys are doing. I know this book is about child labor laws, but there are so many kids in this picture. The kids must hate this work they are doing. Not one of them is smiling. I wonder what they would say to me if I were right there with them."
A young girl is standing with a canvas bag in a field. The caption reads: "Edith, five years old."	"Here's a very little girl standing in a field. The caption says she's five! Wow! That's young! She is holding a big bag, and she has no shoes on. I bet she has to fill that bag with something from the field. I bet she doesn't get paid for doing all this work. She looks poor, and her little feet must really be hurting her. I wonder what she would say to the people who made her do this kind of work. I know that the author is sharing his thinking about child labor laws through his words and selected photos. He is doing so in the form of a persuasive monologue, which allows him to present his perspective on this topic. I know that monologues—a presentation of one person's views—which are often shared through plays, opera, animated cartoons, prose fiction, and film, are designed to influence the recipient's thinking—in this case, my thinking. I want to know more about child labor laws, so I'll just search online for additional sources."

Ms. Johnson shows her students how she types in "history of child labor laws" as a Google search. Then she thinks aloud as she reads through all the articles. She finds one she likes: www.history.com/topics/child-labor. This article also has links titled Labor Day, Labor Movement, Strikes, and Industrial Revolution.	"Now here's an article about child labor laws. As I skim through this site, the word strikes pops out for me. I know a little about strikes. I wonder if children participated in strikes just like I've seen adults do today. I'm going to click on this, and then skim it to see if it is really related to my topic, and also see what new information I can find. The book I was reading and looking at didn't mention child strikes, so I wonder if this source of information will tell me more."

they are developing insights about child labor in America and also about the role of monologue in presenting one's beliefs. Here's an example of how she scaffolds the understanding of two students who are working as partners. Notice how she uses picture clues to help them better understand.

GINA: I don't know what the kids would say to each other.

PATTY: Yeah, me neither.

GINA: I never saw a kid who worked in a place like that.

MS. JOHNSON: (noticing the students need for assistance) So, you've never seen a place that looked like that?

GINA: Well, I've seen dirty places before, but I've never seen kids working in dirty places.

MS. JOHNSON: Why don't you think for a minute what it would be like if you two worked there, in this dirty place.

GINA: Yuck!

PATTY: Ew! My nails!

MS. JOHNSON: What do you mean by that?

GINA: Well, I wouldn't want to work there.

MS. JOHNSON: What would you say to each other if you had to work there?

PATTY: I would tell you that this place is dirty and unsafe.

GINA: Yeah, kids shouldn't be working around all this dangerous, dirty equipment.

PATTY: We could get hurt.

MS. JOHNSON: What do you mean?

PATTY: Well, this looks like work for an adult—a strong adult who knows what he's doing.

GINA: That's for sure. This is no place for a kid. Kids should be outside playing, not working like that.

PATTY: I would also think about escaping this kind of work. I wonder if there is some other job I could do that isn't so dirty and unsafe.

MS. JOHNSON: Good. So what you two have done is thought about perspective and what it would be like to be the two boys in this photo. You noticed the entire photo, the dirty, unsafe environment, and you thought about what it would be like to be those two boys. By looking at the visuals and thinking about perspective, you can think more critically about the text. It might make more sense to do this as you continue to read the book together.

Next, using the dialogue between these two students, Ms. Johnson models for them how to use online sources to expand their base of knowledge. The conversation continues:

MS. JOHNSON: So you two have talked a lot about how unsafe and dangerous this environment is for kids.

PATTY: It sure is!

MS. JOHNSON: What are you thinking about right now? What wonderings do you have about what you are reading and looking at so far?

GINA: I wonder if all the kids worked in unsafe, dangerous jobs . . . or was it just this girl?

MS. JOHNSON: Terrific, so you're wondering if child labor practices were widespread, meaning lots of kids were involved. Let's turn to our online resources to find out. We're lucky to have a world of information at our fingertips. Watch me as I search for a related article.

Ms. Johnson searches on "child labor unsafe dangerous jobs" and comes across the site www.childlaborphotoproject.org/childlabor.html, which has many hyperlinks at the top of the page.

MS. JOHNSON: Let's see. This site is organized much like a table of contents. I know this by looking at the top (pointing to all of the possible links). Here's a link that says "Frequently Asked Questions about child labor." I think this one might give us some more information, because it probably answers all of the questions we have (clicks on link). Great! It says, "What do child laborers do?" I'm going to click on this.

PATTY: Yeah! This is like a table of contents or an index.

GINA: Yep! Except there are no page numbers.

MS. JOHNSON: That's right. So after clicking on "What do child laborers do?" I will skim and scan to see if any words pop out for me. What kind of words might we be looking for?

GINA: *Dangerous.* Or maybe the word *unsafe.*

MS. JOHNSON: That's right! Look here, it says "risky." Let me read this: "Being a maid in someone's house can be risky. Child maids are typically cut off from friends and family and can easily be physically abused."

PATTY: Oh, wow!

GINA: That is so sad.

MS. JOHNSON: Yes, it is. So by searching a little more, we are seeing additional cases of children working in unsafe environments. There's a lot of information on most topics, and we can find it by looking in books and online to find the answers. This is what real reading involves. It answers the questions *you* initially have and also new ones you get as you read.

PATTY: I know! No one told me to look up that question. Wait, wait—I have another question!

As this interaction illustrates, it is during guided practice that Ms. Johnson is able to differentiate instruction for students as she listens to their conversations and assesses how they are developing their bases of knowledge. With this information, she is able to help them better understand both the topic they are studying and how they can become more independent as learners. During guided practice, if Ms. Johnson finds herself teaching or reteaching certain information or processes to many children, she can again share this information with the whole class before the students begin to engage in collaborative learning experiences. Also, by keeping track of the points she has shared with pairs of students during guided practice, she is able to reassess if the students have gained these understandings as they later work collaboratively. For example, when she later observes Gina and Patty as they work in a collaborative group, she will be sure to notice what strategies they are using to search hyperlinks related to their selected topic of study.

Collaborative Work: Using New Language and Ideas to Complete a Related Task

At this point, the students in Ms. Johnson's class are ready to work collaboratively to gain more background knowledge about child labor laws and author perspective. Realizing that the students have a basic understanding of the topic but are just beginning to understand how to search hyperlinks and to make judgments about source value while simultaneously predicting and inferring the veracity and connectedness of the information, Ms. Johnson decides to model for the entire class how an expert reader uses these skills:

MS. JOHNSON: As I shared when you were doing partner work, I often like to read multiple online sites or hyperlinks when I'm studying a topic. When I look at each site, I have to be real careful to be sure that it is related to my main topic, is telling me something new, and also seems real or authentic. For example, like you, I've been reading a lot about the horrible conditions that children worked in during the early decades of the 20th century. Because, like you, I'm a good reader, I know that when I read I need to pay attention to where the information is coming from. I need to know the author's perspective. Many of these authors of books and articles write and report about the horrible conditions and unhappy children. I wonder if there are any examples of when children were happy with the work that they did.

As Ms. Johnson continues modeling while conversing with her students, her purpose is to illustrate for her students how she searches Google or Bing, how she skims and scans for information, and how she clicks on different hyperlinks to guide her predictions and questions:

MS. JOHNSON: As I skim this article, I see the words *benefits* and *happy*. However, as I read further, I don't see what the specific benefits of child labor are, or any cases of happy children. However, I can *infer* because of these words that there must have been some benefits and some children who were happy to work. As I continue to read, I am *predicting* that the author will be writing about some of the benefits that came of child labor. Ah, here it is (reads aloud). Okay, now I see. The benefits were not for the children *doing* the work but rather the children on the other end. For example, kids worked in mines, which led to children in homes having heat. Another example is when kids worked in unsafe factories making medicine bottles, these medicine bottles were used for the medicine that helped many children and adults get well.

                  As I *evaluate* this text, I'm asking myself, is that really a benefit that justifies kids working in unsafe conditions, for many hours? Hmmm . . . I care about the sick people, but I don't like little kids working in those conditions. The author must be trying to show both sides of this topic. He must be saying that the benefits of all these children working are that other kids, the nonlaborers, receive the benefits. And in this case, it's the heat and medicine. I've heard before that sometimes the benefit does not outweigh the risk. In other words, as I weigh these facts and situations, I'm thinking it's not really worth the dangerous work these kids are doing in order for a few other children to reap the benefit.

In this think-aloud, Ms. Johnson has modeled inferring, predicting, and evaluating while using online text sources. Her purpose has been to ensure that her students can use these comprehension strategies when they research a topic. Even though she had initially modeled this research process before the students began partner work, Ms. Johnson had determined during their guided practice that she needed to model it again for her students. She realizes that as students add a new genre, they often need support in learning to apply all of their comprehension strategies.

Feeling more confident that her students can now use their literacy skills of predicting, inferring, and evaluating, Ms. Johnson invites them to begin their collaborative work by using a graphic organizer to map their thinking as they read multiple sources on a topic (see fig. 5.1). Student groups of four read from their textbook chapter and use one laptop to connect to additional sources about child labor. Ms. Johnson asks the students to read the first few paragraphs of the textbook, synthesize what they read, and then go on an online journey to further their understanding of the topic.

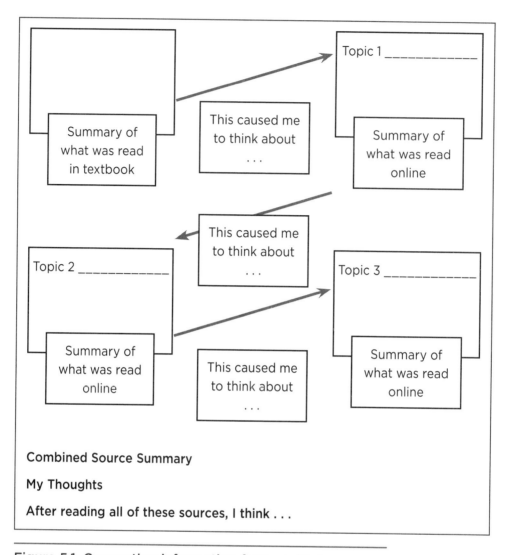

Figure 5.1: Connecting information from multiple sources.

One YouTube site that Ms. Johnson suggests because it incorporates the perspective shown in the Freedman and Hine book is www.youtube.com/watch?v=_tY1gk6J6zc. As her students collaborate, they discover others, such as *Children of the Industrial Revolution* at www.youtube.com/watch?v=E_tFFQy. They also identify many terrific books on this topic, including *Mother Jones: Labor Leader*, by Connie Colwell Miller (2007); *Kids Have Rights Too*, by Janine Scott (2008); and *Kids on Strike*, by Susan Campbell Bartoletti (2003).

In addition to supporting students as they gain proficiency at finding, viewing, and reading these and other related books and sites, Ms. Johnson posts six photographs depicting child labor, which she obtained from Google Images, around the room. She then places a chart next to each photograph. She invites the student groups to visit each photograph, talk about it, and write on the charts what the children in the photo might be thinking and what questions they might ask the children (see fig. 5.2).

	What might the children be thinking?	What questions would I ask the children?

Figure 5.2: What are we thinking?

Students are given approximately five to seven minutes to view, discuss, and write about a photograph before moving on to the next one. When they finish the last station, Ms. Johnson gives the groups additional time to read through the ideas on one poster and synthesize the information in preparation for sharing with the whole class. As the groups share their photo and the accompanying information on the chart, the rest of the class takes notes using a Foldable graphic organizer, asks questions, and converses about the photo. As shown in figure 5.3 (page 135), on the top flap of the Foldable, which is cut into six sections, students sketch the image. On the inside flap, students take notes from the group that is sharing the information.

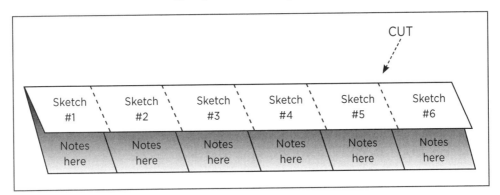

Figure 5.3: Note-taking Foldable.

Independent Work: Transferring the Newly Acquired Information to Novel Tasks

After all the groups have disseminated the information from the charts and photos, Ms. Johnson asks the students to choose one of the photos or to go online to find another they prefer. She then asks them to independently write a monologue in which they take the perspective of one of the children in the photos and share where they work, what kind of work they have to do, how they are treated, and how this kind of work makes them feel. The intent of the monologue is to persuade the listener that child labor is either a positive or negative practice.

Once they have written their monologues, the students are free to find another classmate who shares their views and to work again as partners to choose a medium and develop a format for sharing their monologues with the whole class, such as a speech, a YouTube video, or a PhotoBooth presentation. Many students enjoy performing their monologues using a green screen and a video recorder. The following website gives a step-by-step plan for using a green screen in your classroom: http://blogs.scholastic.com/3_5/2008/08/movie-making-ma.html.

Ms. Johnson asks her students to participate in many whole-class performances and presentations because she wants to give them opportunities to use their developing academic and topical language and their performance and technology skills. In classrooms where time is an issue and whole-class performances aren't always feasible, individuals or partners can present to another individual or partner team.

Younger Students and Online Research

By using a gradual release of responsibility model with children at any grade level, a teacher can model how to apply one's reading skills to the reading of hyperlinked texts. For example, in a first-grade class, a teacher who is exploring a topic such as communities with her students could model the process and support students as they read together. The teacher could use a common text, like the social studies textbook, to begin the conversation. Prior to reading the text, the teacher could fill in a KWL chart to show students all they know about communities and what they wonder about. The wondering column could be a springboard for further research.

For example, if students wonder what kinds of community jobs are dangerous, the teacher could model searching such a topic online by using a computer and projector. During the teacher's search, she would be sure to model what is involved in thinking about questions surrounding a given topic. She would use sentence frames such as the following: "As I am reading about different community jobs in this book, I'm wondering, what are some community jobs that also help people? I think I will search this online and find out more about jobs that help people. I will be sure to look for some hyperlinks, or words and phrases that may be a different color or underlined, because that might give me additional information."

Because one of the challenges of online research for students in primary grades is the readability of the text, the teacher could model for students how to use the Google Images feature to find a variety of images about a topic. Students can gain a lot of information about a topic by using visual as well as written information. The image in figure 5.4 could be found during a teacher think-aloud searching for the topic of "dangerous community jobs."

Figure 5.4: Image from a search on "dangerous community jobs."

Conclusion

If we could turn the clock back to about 1994, we would be reminded that the World Wide Web was a pretty new concept. Think about how the continuing growth of the Internet has transformed our lives. Did you ever imagine that you would have not one, but perhaps even a bank of computers in your classroom? When did you get your first iPod or smart phone? Do you ever wonder how you functioned without these devices?

Now, fast-forward three years. What will have changed because of technology? While that's just a few years away, we wonder, because of technology's ability to bring about quick changes, how our economy, energy and food sources, and especially education will be affected during those few short years. When we hear the term *book*, will we think only of electronic books? Will students be reading ebooks from computers that are only as big as an iPad? Will there be more distance learning opportunities connected to our classrooms? It's intriguing but difficult to make these predictions, because we are teachers, not computer engineers.

The only predictions the three of us feel safe making are that there are way more changes to come and that these changes will be highly intriguing to students and to us. Judging from the technological advances we've witnessed thus far, students will most likely continue to have ever-expanding tools and resources for learning. While such advances are equally motivating to most students, the opportunity to engage with technology is not yet equally available to all. Therefore, as educators we are tasked with preparing students to participate in a world that we cannot yet fathom, but one that will offer increasing opportunities to acquire information from digitally driven sources. To meet this challenge means capturing students' motivation to learn via Web 2.0 tools and coupling this with instruction that gives all students opportunities to experience new-media texts as an avenue to learn individually and collaboratively, and to share their learning.

To help accomplish this exciting challenge, we have attempted to draw from all that we as a field know about teaching and learning and to use this knowledge to illustrate the importance of text-supported thinking and collaboration. Additionally, we have offered instructional examples across the grades to support reader and text interactions and have illustrated that intentional instruction and learning can occur in many contexts via a wide array of texts. It is vital that as we continue to expand our notions of what it means to be literate in the 21st century, we also continually reaffirm what we know as best practice and use it to support explorations for new practice and learning.

References and Resources

Adler, M. J., & Van Doren, C. (1972). *How to read a book*. New York: Touchstone. (Original work published 1940)

Albers, P. (2007). *Finding the artist within: Creating and reading visual texts in English language arts classrooms*. Newark, DE: International Reading Association.

Alexie, S. (2007). *The absolutely true diary of a part-time Indian*. New York: Little, Brown.

Allard, H. (1977). *Miss Nelson is missing!* New York: Houghton Mifflin.

Allington, R. L., & Johnston, P. H. (2002). *Reading to learn: Lessons from exemplary fourth-grade classrooms*. New York: Guilford.

Alvermann, D. E., Young, J. P., Weaver, D., Hinchman, K. A., Moore, D. W., Phelps, S. F., et al. (1996). Middle and high school students' perceptions of how they experience text-based discussions: A multicase study. *Reading Research Quarterly*, *31*(3), 244–267.

An, N. (2002). *A step from heaven*. Asheville, NC: Front Street.

Anderson, M. T. (2004). *Feed*. New York: Candlewick.

Anderson, R. C., & Pearson, P. D. (1984). A schema-theoretic view of basic processes in reading. In P. D. Pearson, R. Barr, M. L. Kamil, & P. Mosenthal (Eds.), *Handbook of Reading Research* (pp. 255–291). White Plains, NY: Longman.

Applebee, A. N., Langer, J. A., Nystrand, M., & Gamoran, A. (2003). Discussion-based approaches to developing understanding: Classroom instruction and student performance in middle and high school English. *American Educational Research Journal*, *40*(3), 685–730.

Armbruster, B. B., Anderson, T. H., Armstrong, J. O., Wise, M. A., Janisch, C., & Meyer, L. (1991). Reading and questioning in content area lessons. *Journal of Reading Behavior*, *23*, 35–60.

Asher, J. (2007). *Thirteen reasons why*. New York: Penguin Books.

Balliett, B. (2010). *The Calder game*. New York: Scholastic.

Bartoletti, S .C. (2003). *Kids on strike*. New York: Sandpiper.

Bean, J. C., Chappell, V. A., & Gillam, A. M. (2011). *Reading rhetorically* (3rd ed.). Boston: Longman.

Beck, I. L., McKeown, M. G., & Kucan, L. (2002). *Bringing words to life: Robust vocabulary instruction*. New York: Guilford.

Beck, I. L., Perfetti, C. A., & McKeown, M. G. (1982). Effects of long term vocabulary instruction on lexical access and reading comprehension. *Journal of Educational Psychology, 74*, 506–521.

Biggs, A., Hagins, W. C., Holliday, W. G., Kapicka, C. L., Lundgren, L., MacKenzie, A., et al. (2007). *Glencoe science biology*. New York: Glencoe McGraw-Hill.

Blackboard (2010). *Education in the 21st century*. Accessed at www.blackboard .com/Markets/K-12/Learn-for-K12/Leadership-Views/Education-in-the-21st-Century.aspx on April 3, 2011

Blau, S. (1994). Transactions between theory and practice in the teaching of literature. In J. Flood & J. A. Langer (Eds.), *Literature instruction: Practice and policy* (pp. 19–52). New York: Scholastic.

Bluestein, N. A. (2010). Unlocking text features for determining importance in expository text: A strategy for struggling readers. *Reading Teacher, 63*(7), 597–600.

Blum, I. H., Koskinen, P. S., Bhartiya, P., & Hluboky, S. (2010). Thinking and talking about books: Using prompts to stimulate discussion. *Reading Teacher, 63*(6), 495–499.

Blumenthal, K. (2002). *Six days in October: The stock market crash of 1929*. New York: Atheneum.

Bohn, C. M., Roehrig, A. D., & Pressley, M. (2004). The first days of school in the classrooms of two more effective and four less effective primary-grades teachers. *Elementary School Journal, 104*(4), 269–288.

Bourke, R. T. (2008). First graders and fairy tales: One teacher's action research of critical literacy. *Reading Teacher, 62*(4), 304–312.

Boyne, John. (2007). *The boy in the striped pajamas*. New York: Random House.

Britton, J. (1983). Writing and the story of the world. In B. Kroll & E. Wells (Eds.), *Explorations in the development of writing theory, research, and practice* (pp. 3–30). New York: Wiley.

Brown, A. L., & Campione, J. C. (1990). Communities of learning and thinking, or a context by any other name. *Contributions to Human Development, 21*, 108–126.

Calkins, L. M. (1994). *The art of teaching writing: New edition*. Portsmouth, NH: Heinemann.

Carroll, L. (1996). *Through the looking-glass: Complete and unabridged*. New York: Penguin. (Original work published 1872)

Cassidy, J. (1994). *Earthsearch: A kid's geography museum in a book*. Palo Alto, CA: Klutz.

Cazden, C. B. (2001). *Classroom discourse: The language of teaching and learning.* Portsmouth, NH: Heinemann.

Chowning, J. T., & Fraser, P. (2007). *An ethics primer.* Seattle WA: Northwest Association of Biomedical Research. Accessed at www.nwabr.org/education /pdfs/PRIMER/PrimerPieces/SocSem.pdf.

Cisneros, S. (1991). *Woman hollering creek and other stories.* New York: Random House.

Clarke, P. J., Snowling, M. J., Truelove, E., & Hulme, C. (2010). Ameliorating children's reading-comprehension difficulties: A randomized controlled trial. *Psychological Science, 21*(8), 1106–1116.

Coiro, J., & Dobler, B. (2007). Exploring the online comprehension strategies used by sixth-grade skilled readers to search for and locate information on the Internet. *Reading Research Quarterly, 42*(2), 214–257.

Coleman, D. (2010, October). *Understanding the Common Core Standards in English language arts.* Paper presented at the annual meeting of the Iowa Council of Teachers of English, Johnson, IA.

Colvin, G., & Lazar, M. (1995). Establishing classroom routines. In A. Deffenbaugh, G. Sugai, & G. Tindal (Eds.), *The Oregon Conference Monograph 1995* (Vol. 7, pp. 209–212). Eugene: University of Oregon.

Common Core State Standards Initiative. (2010). *Common Core State Standards for English language arts & literacy in history/social studies, science, and technical subjects.* Accessed at www.corestandards.org/assets/CCSSI_ELA%20Standards .pdf on March 28, 2011.

Cordón, L. A., & Day, J. D. (1996). Strategy use on standardized reading comprehension tests. *Journal of Educational Psychology, 88,* 288–295.

Creech, S. (2001). *Love that dog.* New York: HarperCollins.

Cronin, D. (2000). *Click, clack, moo: Cows that type.* New York: Simon & Schuster.

Cullinan, B. E. (1989). *Literature and the child* (2nd ed.). San Diego, CA: Harcourt Brace Jovanovich.

Cunningham, J. (1982). Generating interactions between schemata and text. In J. Niles & L. Harris (Eds.), *New inquiries in reading research and instruction: Thirty-first yearbook of the National Reading Conference* (pp. 42–47). Rochester, NY: National Reading Conference.

Daniels, H. (1994). *Literature circles: Voice and choice in the student-centered classroom.* York, ME: Stenhouse.

Daniels, H. (2002). *Literature circles: Voice and choice in book clubs and reading groups.* York, ME: Stenhouse.

Daniels, P. (1999). *Oceans.* Washington, DC: National Geographic Society.

Davey, B. (1983). Think-aloud: Modeling the cognitive processed of reading comprehension. *Journal of Reading, 27*(1), 44–47.

Davidson, C. N., & Goldberg, D. T. (2009). *The future of learning institutions in a digital age.* Cambridge, MA: MIT Press.

dePaola, T. (2000). *Nana upstairs and Nana downstairs.* New York: Putnam.

DiCamillo, K. (2000). *Because of Winn-Dixie.* Somerville, MA: Candlewick Press.

DiGisi, L. L., & Willett, J. B. (1995). What high school biology teachers say about their textbook use: A descriptive study. *Journal of Research in Science Teaching, 32,* 123–142.

Dobson, T. M. (2007a). Constructing (and deconstructing) reading through hypertext: Literature and the new media. In A. Adams & S. Brindley (Eds.), *Teaching secondary English with ICT.* Maidenhead, Berkshire, UK: Open University Press.

Dobson, T. M. (2007b, May). *Reading wikis: E-literature and the negotiation of reader/ writer roles.* Paper presented at the annual meeting of the Canadian Society for Studies in Education, Winnipeg, MB.

Driscoll, M. (2004). *A child's introduction to the night sky: The story of the stars, planets, and constellations—and how you can find them in the sky.* New York: Black Dog & Leventhal.

Duke, N. K. (2000). 3.6 minutes a day: The scarcity of informational texts in first grade. *Reading Research Quarterly, 35*(2), 202–224.

Duke, N. K. (2010). The real-world reading and writing U.S. children need. *Phi Delta Kappan, 91*(5), 68–71.

Duke, N. K., & Bennett-Armistead, V. S. (2003). *Reading and writing informational text in the primary grades.* New York: Scholastic.

Durrell, D. D. (1956). *Improving reading instruction.* Yonkers-on-Hudson, NY: World Book.

Dymock, S. (2005). Teaching expository text structure awareness. *Reading Teacher, 59*(2), 177–182.

Dyson, A. H. (2001). Relational sense and textual sense in a U.S. urban classroom: The contested case of Emily, girlfriend of a ninja. In B. Comber & A. Simpson (Eds.), *Negotiating critical literacies in classrooms* (pp. 3–17). Mahwah, NJ: Erlbaum.

Dyson, A. H. (2006). On saying it right (write): "Fix-its" in the foundations of learning to write. *Research in the Teaching of English, 41,* 8–44.

Earle, R. A. (1969). Use of the structured overview in mathematics classes. In H. L. Herber & P. L. Sanders (Eds.), *Research in reading in the content areas* (pp. 49–58). Syracuse, NY: Syracuse Reading and Language Arts Center.

Eeds, M., & Wells, D. (1989). Grand conversations: An exploration of meaning construction in literature study groups. *Research in the Teaching of English, 23*(1), 4–29.

Egan, K. (1997). *The educated mind: How cognitive tools shape our understanding.* Chicago: University of Chicago Press.

Fisher, D., Flood, J., Lapp, D., & Frey, N. (2004). Interactive read-alouds: Is there a common set of implementation practices? *Reading Teacher, 58*(1), 8–17.

Fisher, D., & Frey, N. (2007). *Checking for understanding: Formative assessment techniques for your classroom.* Alexandria, VA: Association for Supervision and Curriculum Development.

Fisher, D., & Frey, N. (2008a). *Ancient civilizations in graphic novel.* Columbus, OH: Glencoe McGraw-Hill.

Fisher, D., & Frey, N. (2008b). *Better learning for structured teaching: A framework for the gradual release of structured responsibility.* Alexandria, VA: Association for Supervision and Curriculum Development.

Fisher, D., & Frey, N. (2008c). *Word wise and content rich, grades 7–12: Five essential steps to teaching academic vocabulary.* Portsmouth, NH: Heinemann.

Fisher, D., & Frey, N. (2009). *Background knowledge: The missing piece of the comprehension puzzle.* Portsmouth, NH: Heinemann.

Fisher, D., & Frey, N. (2011). *Improving adolescent literacy: Content area strategies at work* (3rd ed.). Boston: Allyn & Bacon.

Fisher, D., Frey, N., & Lapp, D. (2008a). *In a reading state of mind: Brain research, teacher modeling, and comprehension instruction.* Newark, DE: International Reading Association.

Fisher, D., Frey, N., & Lapp, D. (2008b). Shared readings: Modeling comprehension, vocabulary, text structures, and text features for older readers. *Reading Teacher, 61,* 548–557.

Fitzgerald, F. S. (1925). *The great Gatsby.* New York: C. Scribner's Sons.

Fitzgerald, F. S. (1945). *The crack-up.* New York: New Directions.

Flake, S. (1998). *The skin I'm in.* New York: Hyperion.

Flood, J., & Lapp, D. (1995). Broadening the lens: Towards an expanded conceptualization of literacy. In K. Hinchman, D. Leu, & D. Kinzer (Eds.), *Perspectives on literacy research and practice* (pp. 1–6). Chicago: National Reading Conference.

Fountas, I. C., & Pinnell, G. S. (2001). *Guiding readers and writers: Teaching comprehension, genre, and content literacy.* Portsmouth, NH: Heinemann.

Freedman, R. (1994). *Kids at work: Lewis Hine and the crusade against child labor.* New York: Houghton Mifflin.

Freedman, R. (2000). *Give me liberty! The story of the Declaration of Independence.* New York: Holiday House.

Fremon, D. K. (2000). *The Jim Crow laws and racism in American history.* Berkeley Heights, NJ: Enslow.

Frey, N., & Fisher, D. (2006). *Language arts workshop: Purposeful reading and writing instruction.* Upper Saddle River, NJ: Merrill Prentice Hall.

Frey, N., & Fisher, D. (2011). Structuring the talk: Ensuring academic conversations matter. *Clearing House, 84*(1), 15–20.

Frey, N., Fisher, D., & Berkin, A. (2008). *Good habits, great readers: Building the literacy community.* Boston: Allyn & Bacon.

Frey, N., Fisher, D., & Gonzalez, A. (2010). *Literacy 2.0: Reading and writing in 21st century classrooms.* Bloomington, IN: Solution Tree Press.

Gainer, J., & Lapp, D. (2010). *Literacy remix: Bridging adolescents' in and out of school literacies.* Newark, DE: International Reading Association.

Galindo, R., Tierney, R. J., & Stowell, L. (1989). Multimedia and multilayers in multiple texts. In S. McCormick & J. Zutell (Eds.), *Cognitive and social perspectives for literacy research and instruction* (pp. 311–321). Chicago: National Reading Conference.

Giles, G. (2002). *Shattering glass.* Brookfield, CT: Roaring Book Press.

Giorgis, C., & Johnson, N. J. (2002). Multiple perspectives. *Reading Teacher, 55*(5), 486–494.

Gipson, F. (1995). *Old Yeller.* New York: HarperTrophy. (Original work published 1956)

Gow, M. (2002). *Tycho Brahe: Astronomer.* Berkeley Heights, NJ: Enslow.

Graff, G., & Birkenstein, C. (2006). *They say/I say: The moves that matter in academic writing.* New York: W. W. Norton.

Graves, M. F. (2006). *The vocabulary book: Learning & instruction.* New York: Teachers College Press.

Guthrie, J. T., & Wigfield, A. (2000). Engagement and motivation in reading. In M. L. Kamil, P. B. Mosenthal, P. D. Pearson, & R. Barr (Eds.), *Handbook of Reading Research* (vol. 3, pp. 403–422). Mahwah, NJ: Erlbaum.

Haddon, M. (2003). *The curious incident of the dog in the night-time.* New York: Random House.

Hadjioannou, X. (2007). Bringing the background to the foreground: What do classroom environments that support authentic discussions look like? *American Educational Research Journal, 44*(2), 370–399.

Hansen, J. (2001). *When writers read* (2nd ed.). Portsmouth, NH: Heinemann.

Hemingway, E. (1996). *The old man and the sea* [Introduction by H. Bloom]. Broomall, PA: Chelsea House. (Original work published 1952)

Herber, H. L. (1970). *Teaching reading in the content areas*. Upper Saddle River, NJ: Prentice Hall.

Hesse, K. (1998). *The music of the dolphins*. New York: Scholastic.

Heuvel, E. (2009a). *A family secret*. New York: Farrar, Straus and Giroux.

Heuvel, E. (2009b). *The search*. New York: Farrar, Straus and Giroux.

Hiebert, E. H. (2005). In pursuit of an effective, efficient vocabulary curriculum for elementary students. In E. H. Hiebert & M. L. Kamil (Eds.), *Teaching and learning vocabulary: Bringing research to practice* (pp. 243–263). Mahwah, NJ: Erlbaum.

Hillocks, G., Jr. (2010). Teaching argument for critical thinking and writing: An introduction. *English Journal, 99*(6), 24–32.

Hinton, S. E. (1967). *The outsiders*. New York: Dell.

Hobbs, R. (2004). Analyzing advertising in the English language arts classroom: A quasi-experimental study. *Studies in Media & Literacy Education, 4*(2), 1–4.

Hobbs, R. (2007). *Reading the media in high school: Media literacy in high school English*. New York: Teachers College Press.

Hobbs, R., & Frost, R. (2003). Measuring the acquisition of media-literacy skills. *Reading Research Quarterly, 38*, 330–356.

Howe, J. (2001). *The misfits*. New York: Aladdin.

Howell, C. H. (1993). *Reptiles and amphibians*. Washington, DC: National Geographic.

Hull, G. A., & Nelson, M. E. (2005). Locating the semiotic power of multimodality. *Written Communication, 22*, 224–262.

Iggulden, C., & Iggulden, H. (2007). *The dangerous book for boys*. New York: William Morrow.

Innocenti, R. (1985). *Rose blanche*. New York: Harcourt Brace.

Iser, W. (1978). *The act of reading: A theory of aesthetic response*. Baltimore: Johns Hopkins University Press.

Ivey, G., & Fisher, D. (2006). When thinking skills trump reading skills. *Educational Leadership, 64*(2), 16–21.

Johnston, P. (2004). *Choice words: How our language affects children's learning*. York, ME: Stenhouse.

Kafka, F. (1946). *The metamorphosis*. New York: Vanguard Press.

Keefer, M. W., Zeitz, C. M., & Resnick, L. B. (2000). Judging the quality of peer-led student dialogues. *Cognition and Instruction, 18*, 53–81.

Kinney, J. (2007). *Diary of a wimpy kid*. New York: Amulet Books.

Knickerbocker, J. L. & Rycik, J. (2002). Growing into literature: Adolescents' literary interpretation and appreciation. *Journal of Adolescent & Adult Literacy, 46*(3), 196–208.

Konigsberg, E. L. (1967). *From the mixed-up files of Mrs. Basil E. Frankweiler.* New York: Atheneum.

Kress, G. (2003). *Literacy in the new media age.* New York: Routledge.

Kress, G., & van Leeuwen, T. (1996/2006). *Reading images: The grammar of visual design* (1st and 2nd eds.). New York: Routledge.

Labov, W. (1995). The case of the missing copula: The interpretation of zeros in African American English. In L. Gleitman & M. Liberman (Eds.), *Languge: An invitation to cognitive science* (2nd ed., vol. 1, pp. 25–54). Cambridge, MA: MIT Press.

Langer, J. A. (1985). A sociocognitive view of literacy learning. *Research in the Teaching of English, 19*(4), 235–247.

Langer, J. A. (1987). A sociocognitive perspective on literacy. In J. A. Langer (Ed.), *Language, literacy, and culture: Issues of society and schooling* (pp. 1–20). Norwood, NJ: Ablex.

Langer, J. A. (1994). Reader-based literature instruction. In J. Flood & J. A. Langer (Eds.), *Literature instruction: Practice and policy* (pp. 1–18). New York: Scholastic.

Langer, J. A. (1995). *Envisioning literature: Literary understanding and literature instruction.* New York: Teachers College Press.

Lankshear, C., & Knobel, M. (2003). *New literacies: changing knowledge and classroom learning.* Philadelphia: Open University Press.

Lapp, D., & Fisher, D. (2009a). *Essential readings on comprehension.* Newark, DE: International Reading Association.

Lapp, D., & Fisher, D. (2009b). It's all about the book: Motivating teens to read. *Journal of Adolescent & Adult Literacy, 52*, 556–651.

Lapp, D., Fisher, D., & Johnson, K. (2010). Text mapping plus: Improving comprehension through supported retellings. *Journal of Adolescent & Adult Literacy, 53*(5), 423–426.

Lapp, D., Flood, J., & Fisher, D. (1999). Intermediality: How the use of multiple media enhances learning. *Reading Teacher, 52*(7), 776–780.

Lee, H. (1960). *To kill a mockingbird.* New York: J. B. Lippincott.

Lemke, D. (2010). *Good vs. evil: The awakening.* New York: Stone Arch.

London, J. (1990). *The call of the wild.* New York: Dover. (Original work published 1903)

Lucca, M. (2001). *Where does the water go?* Washington, DC: National Geographic Society.

Macaulay, D. (2003). *Mosque*. Boston: Houghton Mifflin Co.

Martin, R. (1998). *The rough-face girl*. New York: Putnam.

McGinley, W. J., & Denner, P. R. (1987). Story impressions: A prereading/writing activity. *Journal of Reading, 31*(3), 248–253.

McKoon, G., & Ratcliff, R. (1992). Inference during reading. *Psychological Review, 99*(3), 440–466.

Mehan, H. (1979). *Learning lessons: Social organization in the classroom*. Boston, MA: Harvard University Press.

Melville, H. (1963). *Moby-Dick* [Introduction by Sherman Paul]. New York: Dutton. (Original work published 1851)

Michaels, S., O'Connor, C., & Resnick, L. B. (2008). Deliberative discourse idealized and realized: Accountable talk in the classroom and in civic life. *Studies in Philosophy and Education, 27*(4), 283–297.

Miller, C. C. (2007). *Mother Jones: Labor leader*. New York: Capstone Press.

Morrow, L. M., Pressley, M., Smith, J. K., & Smith, M. (1997). The effect of a literature-based program integrated into literacy and science instruction with children from diverse backgrounds. *Reading Research Quarterly, 32*(1), 55–76.

Moss, B. (2003). *Exploring the literature of fact: Children's nonfiction trade books in the elementary classroom*. New York: Guilford Press.

Moss, B. (2004). Teaching expository text structures through information trade book retellings. *Reading Teacher, 57*(8), 710–718.

Moss, B. (2009). The information text gap: The mismatch between non-narrative text types in basal readers and 2009 NAEP recommended guidelines. *Journal of Literacy Research, 40*(2), 201–219.

Munsch, R. (1992). *The paper bag princess*. Toronto, ON: Ammick.

Myers, M. (1996). *Changing our minds: Negotiating English and literacy*. Urbana, IL: National Council of Teachers of English.

National Governors Association. (2010). *Key parts of the English language arts standards. Common Core State Standards Initiative*. Accessed at www.corestandards .org/assets/KeyPointsELA.pdf on March 7, 2010.

Nelson, P. (2003). *Left for dead: A young man's search for justice for the USS Indianapolis*. New York: Delacorte.

New Media Consortium. (2005). *A global imperative: The report of the 21st century literacy summit*. Accessed at http://archive.nmc.org/projects/literacy/index.shtml on August 1, 2010.

Newkirk, T. (2010). The case for slow reading. *Educational Leadership, 67*(6), 6–11.

Nicholson, D. M. (2005). *Remember WWII: Kids who survived tell their stories.* Washington, DC: National Geographic Society.

Nussbaum, E. M. (2008). Collaborative discourse, argumentation, and learning: Preface and literature review. *Contemporary Educational Psychology, 33,* 345–359.

Nystrand, M. (1997). Dialogic instruction: When recitation becomes conversation. In M. Nystrand, A. Gamoran, R. Kachur, & C. Prendergast (Eds.), *Opening dialogue: Understanding the dynamics of language and learning in the English classroom* (pp. 1–29). New York: Teachers College Press.

Ogbu, J. U. (2003). *Black American students in an affluent suburb: A study of academic disengagement.* Mahwah, NJ: Erlbaum.

Orgill, R. (1997). *If I only had a horn: Young Louis Armstrong.* New York: Houghton Mifflin.

Palincsar, A. S., & Brown, A. L. (1984). Reciprocal teaching of comprehension-fostering and comprehension-monitoring activities. *Cognition and Instruction, 1*(2), 117–175.

Paris, S. G., Wasik, B. A., & Turner, J. C. (1991). The development of strategic readers. In R. Barr, M. Kamil, P. Mosenthal, & P. D. Pearson (Eds.), *Handbook of reading research* (2nd ed., pp. 609–640). New York: Longman.

Pauk, W. (1974). *How to study in college.* Boston: Houghton Mifflin.

Pearson, P. D. (2001). *What we have learned in 30 years.* Paper presented at the annual meeting of the National Reading Conference, San Antonio, TX.

Polacco, P. (2000). *The butterfly.* New York: Philomel Books.

Powell, P. H. (2006). *Frog brings rain.* Flagstaff, AZ: Salina Bookshelf.

Prelutsky, J. (1999). *The 20th century children's poetry treasury.* New York: Knopf.

Prensky, M. (2001). Listen to the natives. *Educational Leadership, 63*(4), 8–13.

Pressley, M. (2000). What should comprehension instruction be the instruction of? In M. L. Kamil, P. B. Mosenthal, P. D. Pearson, & R. Barr (Eds.), *Handbook of reading research* (vol. 3, pp. 545–561). Mahwah, NJ: Erlbaum.

Pressley, M., & Afflerbach, P. (1995). *Verbal protocols of reading: The nature of constructively responsive reading.* Mahwah, NJ: Erlbaum.

Pressley, M., & El-Dinary, P.B. (1997). What we know about translating comprehension strategies instruction research into practice. *Journal of Learning Disabilities, 30*(5), 486–488.

Pressley, M., Johnson, C. J., Symons, S., McGoldrick, J. A., & Kurita, J. A. (1989). Strategies that improve children's memory and comprehension of text. *Elementary School Journal, 90,* 3–32.

Prose, F. (2006). *Reading like a writer.* New York: Harper Perennial.

Quiller-Couch, A. T. (1918). *Studies in literature*. New York: G. P. Putnam's Sons.

Raphael, T. E., (1986). Teaching question-and-answer-relationships, revisited. *Reading Teacher, 39*(6), 516-522.

Raphael, T. E., Florio-Ruane, S., & George, M. (2001). Book club plus: A conceptual framework to organize literacy instruction. *Language Arts, 79*(2), 159–168.

Rassool, N. (1999). *Literacy for sustainable development in the age of information.* Philadelphia: Multilingual Matters.

Resnick, L. (2000). Making America smarter. *Education Week, 18*(40), 38–40.

Rex, L., Thomas, E. E., & Engel, S. (2010). Applying Toulmin: Teaching logical reasoning and argumentative writing. *English Journal, 99*(6), 56–62.

Rice, A. (1984). *The master of rampling gate.* New York: Redbook Magazine.

Richardson, W. (2006). *Blogs, wikis and podcasts.* Thousand Oaks, CA: Corwin Press.

Ringgold, F. (1999). *If a bus could talk: The story of Rosa Parks.* New York: Simon & Schuster.

Rosenblatt, L. M. (1978). *The reader, the text, the poem: The transactional theory of the literary work.* Carbondale: Southern Illinois University.

Rosenblatt, L. M. (1995). *Literature as exploration* (5th ed.). New York: Modern Language Association.

Rosenstiel, T. (2008, August 20). *The how vs. where of news consumption. Journalism. org: Pew Research Center's Project for Excellence in Journalism.* Accessed at www .journalism.org/node/12448 on March 11, 2011.

Roser, N. L., Martinez, M. G., Yokota, J., & O'Neal, S. (Eds.). (2005). *What a character! Character study as a guide to literacy meaning making in grades K–8.* Newark, DE: International Reading Association.

Ross, D., Fisher, D., & Frey, N. (2009). The art of argumentation. *Science and Children, 47*(3), 28–31.

Rowling, J. K. (1997). *Harry Potter and the sorcerer's stone.* New York: Scholastic.

Rowling, J. K. (1999). *Harry Potter and the prisoner of Azkaban.* New York: Scholastic.

Rowling, J. K. (2007). *Harry Potter and the deathly hallows.* New York: Scholastic.

Samuels, S. J. (2007). The DIBELS tests: Is speed of barking at print what we mean by reading fluency? *Reading Research Quarterly, 42*(4), 563–566.

Schanzer, R. (2007). *Gold fever! Tales from the California gold rush.* Washington, DC: National Geographic.

Schleichert, E. (1997). *Fish.* Washington, DC: National Geographic Society.

Sciezka, J. (1996). *The true story of the three little pigs.* New York: Puffin.

Scott, J. A. (2008). *Kids have right too.* New York: Children's Press.

Scott, J. A., Skobel, B. J., & Wells, J. (2008). *The word-conscious classroom: Building the vocabulary readers and writers need.* New York: Scholastic.

Sipe, L. R. (2000). The construction of literary understanding by first and second graders in oral response to picture storybook read-alouds. *Reading Research Quarterly, 35*(2), 252–275.

Sloan, C. (2002). *Bury the dead: Tombs, corpses, mummies, skeletons, and rituals.* Washington, DC: National Geographic Society.

Snicket, L. (1999). *The bad beginning.* New York: Scholastic.

Spiegel, D. L. (1998). Reader response approaches and the growth of readers. *Language Arts, 76*(1), 41–48.

Spiro, R. J. (2006). The "New Gutenberg Revolution": Radical new learning, thinking, teaching, and training with technology. *Educational Technology, 46*(1), 3–4.

Spivey, N. N. (1997). *The constructivist metaphor: Reading, writing, and the making of meaning.* San Diego, CA: Academic Press.

Springer, M. (2007). Dishpan ducks. *The Nation's Report Card: Reading 2007* (NCES 2007-496). Accessed at http://nationsreportcard.gov/reading_2007/r0039.asp

Steinbeck, J. (1992). *The grapes of wrath.* New York: Penguin. (Original work published 1939)

Stenberg, G. (2006). Conceptual and perceptual factors in the picture superiority effect. *European Journal of Cognitive Psychology, 18*, 813–847.

Stevens, L. P., & Bean, T. W. (2007). *Critical literacy: Context, research, and practice in the K-12 classroom.* Thousand Oaks, CA: Sage.

Stewart, T. L. (2008). *The mysterious benedict society.* New York: Little, Brown.

Sturm, B. W. (2003). The information and reading preferences of North Carolina children. *School Library Media Research, 6*(1) [Online journal]. Accessed at www.ala.org/ala/mgrps/divs/aasl/aaslpubsandjournals/slmrb/slmrcontents/volume62003/readingpreferences.cfm on March 28, 2011.

Tasmania Department of Education. (2007). *English learning area: Critical literacy.* Accessed at www.education.tas.gov.au/curriculum/standards/english/english/teachers/critlit

Tatham, B. (2002). *How animals shed their skin.* New York: Franklin Watts.

Taylor, C. (1992). *The house that crack built.* San Francisco: Chronicle Books.

Teague, M. (2002). *Dear Mrs. La Rue: Letters from obedience school.* New York: Scholastic.

Telicki, B. (2007). Astronauts in training. In *Treasures: A reading/language arts program* (pp. 84–85). New York: Macmillan/McGraw-Hill.

Tharp, R. G., & Gallimore, R. (1988). *Rousing minds to life: Teaching, learning, and schooling in social context*. New York: Cambridge University Press.

Tienken, C. H., Goldberg, S., & DiRocco, D. (2009). Questioning the questions. *Kappa Delta Pi Record*, *46*(1), 39–43.

Tierney, R. J. (2009). The agency and artistry of meaning makers within and across digital spaces. In S. E. Israel & G. G. Durry (Eds.), *Handbook of Research on Reading Comprehension* (pp. 261–288). New York: Routledge.

Tierney, R. J., Kieffer, R., Whalin, K., Desai, L., Moss, A. G., Harris, J. E., & Hopper, J. (1997). Assessing the impact of hypertext on learners' architecture of literacy learning spaces in different disciplines: Follow-up studies. *Reading On-line: Electronic Journal of the International Reading Association*. Accessed at www.readingonline.org/research/impact on March 28, 2011.

Tompkins, J. (Ed.). (1980). *Reader-response criticism: From formalism to post-structuralism*. Baltimore: Johns Hopkins University Press.

Toulmin, S. (1958). *The uses of argument*. Cambridge, England: Cambridge University Press.

Twain, M. (2001). *The adventures of Huckleberry Finn*. New York: Penguin. (Original work published 1885)

U.S. National Archives and Records Administration. (2011). *Cartoon analysis worksheet*. Accessed at www.archives.gov/education/lessons/worksheets/cartoon.html on March 23, 2011.

Vacca, R. T., & Vacca, J. L. (2007). *Content area reading: Literacy and learning across the curriculum* (9th ed.). Boston: Allyn & Bacon.

Vanderpool, C. (2010). *Moon over manifest*. New York: Delacorte Press.

Walker, R. (2009). *Human body*. New York: DK Publishing.

Welleck, R., & Warren, A. (1949). *Theory of literature*. New York: Harcourt Brace.

Wells, G., & Wells, J. (1989). Learning to talk and talking to learn. *Theory Into Practice*, *23*(3), 190–196.

Westerfeld, S. (2004). *So yesterday*. New York: Razorbill.

White, E. B. (1952). *Charlotte's web*. New York: Harper & Row.

Willems, M. (2003). *Don't let the pigeon drive the bus!* New York: Hyperion.

Williams, J. P. (1993). Comprehension of students with and without learning disabilities: Identification of narrative themes and idiosyncratic text representations. *Journal of Educational Psychology*, *85*(4), 631–641.

Wood, K. D., Lapp, D., Flood, J., & Taylor, D. B. (2008). *Guiding readers through text: Strategy guides for new times* (2nd ed.). Newark, DE: International Reading Association.

Wysocki, A. (2004). Opening new media to writing: Openings and justifications. In A. Wysocki, J. Johnson-Eilola, C. L. Selfe, & G. Sirc (Eds.), *Writing new media: Theory and applications for expanding the teaching of composition* (pp. 1–42). Logan: Utah State University Press.

Zawilinski, L. (2009). Hot blogging: A framework for blogging to promote higher order thinking. *Reading Teacher, 62*(8), 650–661.

Index

Literacy 2.0: Reading and Writing in 21st Century Classrooms

By Nancy Frey, Douglas Fisher, and Alex Gonzalez

Literacy 2.0 is where traditional literacy and technological literacy meet. Benefit from the authors' extensive experience in secondary literacy 2.0 classrooms. Discover precisely what students need to be taught to become proficient in the literacies associated with information and communication technologies. **BKF373**

Implementing RTI With English Learners

By Douglas Fisher, Nancy Frey, and Carol Rothenberg

Learn why response to intervention (RTI) is the ideal framework for supporting English learners. Follow the application and effectiveness of RTI through classroom examples and the stories of four representative students of varying ages, nationalities, and language proficiency levels. **BKF397**

Rebuilding the Foundation: Effective Reading Instruction for 21st Century Literacy

Edited by Timothy V. Rasinski

Teaching reading is a complex task without a simple formula for developing quality instruction. Rather than build on or alter existing models, this book considers how educators and policymakers might think about rebuilding and reconceptualizing reading education, perhaps from the ground up. **BKF399**

Power Tools for Adolescent Literacy: Strategies for Learning

Jan Rozzelle and Carol Scearce

Power Tools for Adolescent Literacy integrates key strategies from Dr. Robert Marzano's meta-analysis and research from top literacy experts in a comprehensive collection of best practices and powerful literacy tools for middle and high school teachers. **BKF261**